OLD MOOI

HOROSCOPE AND ASTRAL DIARY

CAPRICORN

OLD MOORE'S

HOROSCOPE AND ASTRAL DIARY

♑

CAPRICORN

foulsham
LONDON • NEW YORK • TORONTO • SYDNEY

W. Foulsham & Co. Ltd
for Foulsham Publishing Ltd
The Old Barrel Store, Drayman's Lane, Marlow, Bucks SL7 2FF

Foulsham books can be found in all good bookshops and direct from www.foulsham.com

ISBN: 978-0-572-04683-5

Copyright © 2017 Foulsham Publishing Ltd

A CIP record for this book is available from the British Library

All rights reserved

The Copyright Act prohibits (subject to certain very limited exceptions) the making of copies of any copyright work or of a substantial part of such a work, including the making of copies by photocopying or similar process. Written permission to make a copy or copies must therefore normally be obtained from the publisher in advance. It is advisable also to consult the publisher if in any doubt as to the legality of any copying which is to be undertaken.

Printed in Great Britain by Martins The Printers, Berwick-upon-Tweed

CONTENTS

1	Introduction	6
2	The Essence of Capricorn: Exploring the Personality of Capricorn the Goat	7
3	Capricorn on the Cusp	13
4	Capricorn and its Ascendants	16
5	The Moon and the Part it Plays in your Life	24
6	Moon Signs	28
7	Capricorn in Love	32
8	Venus: The Planet of Love	36
9	Venus through the Zodiac Signs	38
10	The Astral Diary: How the Diagrams Work	42
11	Capricorn: Your Year in Brief	44
12	Capricorn 2018: Diary Pages	45
13	How to Calculate Your Rising Sign	124
14	Rising Signs for Capricorn	125
15	The Zodiac, Planets and Correspondences	127

INTRODUCTION

Astrology has been a part of life for centuries now, and no matter how technological our lives become, it seems that it never diminishes in popularity. For thousands of years people have been gazing up at the star-clad heavens and seeing their own activities and proclivities reflected in the movement of those little points of light. Across centuries countless hours have been spent studying the way our natures, activities and decisions seem to be paralleled by their predictable movements. Old Moore, a time-served veteran in astrological research, continues to monitor the zodiac and has produced the Astral Diary for 2018, tailor-made to your own astrological makeup.

Old Moore's Astral Diary is unique in its ability to get the heart of your nature and to offer you the sort of advice that might come from a trusted friend. It enables you to see in a day-by-day sense exactly how the planets are working for you. The diary section advises how you can get the best from upcoming situations and allows you to plan ahead successfully. There's also room on each daily entry to record your own observations or appointments.

While other popular astrology books merely deal with your astrological 'Sun sign', the Astral Diaries go much further. Every person on the planet is unique and Old Moore allows you to access your individuality in a number of ways. The front section gives you the chance to work out the placement of the Moon at the time of your birth and to see how its position has set an important seal on your overall nature. Perhaps most important of all, you can use the Astral Diary to discover your Rising Sign. This is the zodiac sign that was appearing over the Eastern horizon at the time of your birth and is just as important to you as an individual as is your Sun sign.

It is the synthesis of many different astrological possibilities that makes you what you are and with the Astral Diaries you can learn so much. How do you react to love and romance? Through the unique Venus tables and the readings that follow them, you can learn where the planet Venus was at the time of your birth. It is even possible to register when little Mercury is 'retrograde', which means that it appears to be moving backwards in space when viewed from the Earth. Mercury rules communication, so be prepared to deal with a few setbacks in this area when you see the sign ☿. The Astral Diary will be an interest and a support throughout the whole year ahead.

Old Moore extends his customary greeting to all people of the Earth and offers his age-old wishes for a happy and prosperous period ahead.

THE ESSENCE OF CAPRICORN

Exploring the Personality of Capricorn the Goat

(22ND DECEMBER – 20TH JANUARY)

What's in a sign?

You probably think of yourself as being the least complicated person to be found anywhere. Although this is basically true, that doesn't necessarily mean that everyone understands you quite as well as they might. When faced with the real world you are practical, capable and resourceful. That means that you get on well with whatever needs to be done. Where you might sometimes fall down is in terms of communicating your intentions to the world at large – mostly it doesn't seem all that important to do so. In other words, you are not the world's best talker, and probably don't even want to be.

When it comes to sweeping away the red tape and actually getting down to the task in hand, you are second to none. Dextrous and adaptable in all matters that need your unique logic, you come at all problems with the same determination to sort them out. However, your ruling planet is cold, ponderous Saturn, and that could be where the potential problems start. Although you have a kind heart and a genuine desire to improve the lot of others, your methods are sometimes misunderstood. Some people might think you a little aloof, or even difficult to talk to. You have frequent quiet spells and often seem to be particularly content with your own company. On rare occasions this can leave you isolated.

Sharing what you are with the world at large is the most important factor on the road to a more contented life, though even this isn't certain, because most Capricorn people tend to be fairly happy with being the way they are. All the same, when those around you want to see something actually being done, they will call on you. Success is not hard for you to achieve, particularly in a career sense. You don't mind getting your hands dirty and can usually be relied upon to find ingenious answers when they are most needed.

In matters of love you are sincere and will work long and hard for your family. Romantically speaking you take some time to get going but can be ardent and sincere when you finally do. Routines don't bother you, and you can also learn to be adaptable.

Capricorn resources

You probably don't think of yourself as being the most dynamic person in the world, though you certainly are one of the most capable. When others are looking for answers, even in very practical matters, you are in there sorting things out. It's the nuts and bolts of the world that are most important, and you don't seem to have too much trouble fixing broken things – whether it's the living room chair, or the heart of a dear friend.

Instead of trying to be one of life's exciting go-getters, you are likely to be more comfortable working slowly and steadily, sometimes in the background. But this doesn't mean that you fail to make a positive impression. On the contrary, you are very necessary to those who form a part of your life, and they are ever aware of the important part you play. It isn't given to everyone to be showy and flashy, and in any case even if you forced yourself down such roads you probably wouldn't be at all comfortable in a role that doesn't come naturally to you.

One of your greatest attributes is your dry sense of humour. It's always possible for you to make others laugh, even during the most awkward or difficult situations. When the world looks particularly dark we all need a Capricorn subject along to lighten the load. You make a good colleague, know well how to co-operate and tend to work capably, either as part of a team, or when circumstances dictate, on your own.

Your greatest resource, and the one that has made many Capricorn people famous over the years, is your capacity to keep going. When there is a problem to be solved, a bridge to build, or a family to support under difficult circumstances, you really come into your own. This is probably because you don't understand the meaning of the word failure. You can find ways round any number of obstacles, and remain dependable, even when the world and his dog are falling to pieces. Add to this the fact that you are consistent and reliable and it shouldn't be too hard for you to enjoy being a capable Capricorn.

Beneath the surface

Although you might not appear to be very complicated when viewed from the perspective of those who see you on a daily basis, you are actually very complex. The reason that this is not obvious lies in the fact that you betray very little of your inner mind in your day-to-day interactions with others. In the main they see you as being capable and settled – but how wrong they can be.

The fact is that you are rarely totally sure of yourself. The confidence to get things done disguises how often you shake inside, and especially so if you are forced into the public arena. You probably wouldn't relish having to do any sort of presentation or to be put on the spot in front of individuals you consider to be more dynamic than you are. Despite this there are strong saving graces. Even when times are tough, or when you do feel a little shaky inside, your natural way forward is to keep plugging away. In some respects your zodiac sign may represent one of the bravest of them all. You won't allow yourself to be bettered by anyone, and the more pressure that is put upon you to fail, the greater is your internal desire for success.

In matters of emotion you are complicated and difficult to understand. You view relationships with the same patience that you bring to almost all facets of life. Friends can misuse or even abuse you for a while, but there is a breaking point within Capricorn that appears sudden, and very final. And once you have made up your mind to a particular course of action, there isn't any force in the world that will prevent you from implementing it.

Your natural planetary ruler is Saturn, the Lord of Time. As a result you are inclined to see things in the medium and longer term. You rarely show yourself to be impatient and carefully choose a course of action, using mental processes that usually follow tried and tested paths. You won't be hurried or pushed and will always stick to methods of working that seem to have worked for you in the past. Although this might sometimes make you feel lacking in colour or variety, you almost always get where you want to go. Occasionally your inner mind takes a great leap in logic. This can lead to a sudden change in attitude and actions that will shock the world. And why not? Even Capricorns need to keep people guessing sometimes.

You may not be the easiest person in the world to understand, or to get to know fully. Don't worry. The inner secrecy of your nature is half your appeal.

Making the best of yourself

We all need to realise what makes us tick, and to come to terms with the most comfortable way in which we can react with the world at large. This is just as true for the zodiac sign of Capricorn as it is for any other. But nobody is perfect, so what can you do to use your skills to the full and to get on better with those who share the planet with you?

Well for starters, it wouldn't be a bad idea to let others know what you are doing – and why. In practical situations especially it's sometimes much easier for you simply to get on and finish a task on your own. And despite your capabilities this is probably why you are not the world's best teacher. It's simply less complicated to get something done, and then to move on patiently to the next demand. On the way, however, you might alienate those who would love to be your friends, and to learn from you.

When it comes to emotion you should do your best to explain the way you feel. Building up animosity for days, weeks or even months, doesn't really do anyone a lot of good, not even a Capricorn subject. People can't alter to suit your needs if they don't know what it is you want. For this reason you should always be as honest as you can be, even if this proves to be quite embarrassing at first. Be willing to show your flexible side – and even to create one if necessary. Try doing things the way others want to proceed now and again, despite the fact that you could be convinced that they are wrong in their approach. Allowing those around you the right to fail is important and in the end it will only make you look that much more confident and together when you stoop to pick up the pieces.

As often as proves to be possible you should display the inner smile that burns away inside you. Be willing to let your hair down and have a good time in the company of people who really do want to know that you are happy. Most important of all, share your inner honesty with those who are important to you.

The impressions you give

There is a great disparity between the way you feel about certain situations, and the impression you offer to an unsuspecting world. If you could fully see yourself as others usually see you, it's an odds-on certainty that you would be very surprised. The vast majority of those with whom you live and work see you as being ultra confident, very cool and quite capable. If you find this hard to believe, simply ask the most honest of your friends. It doesn't matter how you feel inside, or that you often have to dig around for answers that don't supply themselves immediately. What counts is the barrier that is placed constantly between your inner mind and your outward persona.

This is very important because it means you could get on in life even better than you may appear to be doing at the moment. Think what a great gift it is rarely to show that you are quaking inside. And when your cool approach means that you find advancement coming your way, you move on to the next set of requirements with the same apparent confidence you had before.

On a less positive note, it is possible that certain of the people with whom you interact on a daily basis could find you somewhat cold and even perhaps a little aloof on occasions. This is not the case, but once again there is a screen between the way you feel and the façade you show to the world at large. And though this barrier can be your best friend, it can also be a powerful enemy, especially in emotional or romantic situations. When circumstances necessitate, it is important that you tell those with whom you share your life exactly how you feel. That allows them to modify their own behaviour to suit your needs.

There may not be a great deal of work to do on altering your approach because in the main you are well liked and certainly respected. All that is really required in any case is an understanding that what you think and the way you act are not necessarily the same thing.

The way forward

Although it's true of course that anyone can make favourable alterations to their life, it's entirely possible that yours is already headed in the right direction generally. Capricorn people are not usually too complicated; they remain modest in their objectives and can achieve their ends through the medium of good ideas and hard work. You may not give the impression of being the most exciting person in the world – and nor do you wish to be. But when it's necessary to come up with the goods, mentally and practically, you don't usually have much trouble doing so.

To be and to remain quietly confident isn't too much to ask from life. Under most circumstances you take on tasks that you know you can achieve, try to be kind to others on the way and don't tend to make too many waves. It probably doesn't bother you too much that there are people around who may not care for you. This is essentially because you are a realist and understand that you won't be everyone's cup of tea.

If there are points within your nature that could be improved with effort they might relate to a certain stubborn streak. There are occasions when you become very determined to achieve a particular objective and you may not always listen to alternatives once you think you know how to proceed. However, since you don't tend to take on tasks that you are not equipped to deal with, what some may call intransigence, you might refer to as self-assurance. It is also possible that you sometimes find it difficult to express your inner feelings, and especially those related to love. You can be somewhat suspicious of the motives of others and may guard yourself a little too carefully as a result.

Try to recognise that there is more than one way to skin a cat, and that you can actually learn and grow through co-operation. You may also need to be willing to take on a greater degree of responsibility at work, even though this might go against the grain for a whole host of reasons. When faced with decisions that have a bearing on the lives of others, seek their counsel and take note of their opinions.

There are times when you can be a little too pessimistic for your own good. It is important to cultivate a cheerful approach, even though your sometimes slightly gloomy attitude is actually revered and smiled at by your friends. You are loyal, hard-working and generally kind. Capricorn may not be the most dynamic of the zodiac signs, but it is hard to fault it all the same.

CAPRICORN ON THE CUSP

Old Moore is often asked how astrological profiles are altered for those people born at either the beginning or the end of a zodiac sign, or, more properly, on the cusps of a sign. In the case of Capricorn this would be on the 22nd of December and for two or three days after, and similarly at the end of the sign, probably from the 18th to the 20th of January. In this year's Astral Diaries, once again, Old Moore sets out to explain the differences regarding cuspid signs.

The Sagittarius Cusp – December 22nd to 24th

Oh, what a lovely person you can be, and how respected you are by the world at large. At its best this is a very fortunate combination because it retains all the practical skills of Capricorn, but the nature is somewhat elevated by the quality of Sagittarius. Nothing much is beyond your capabilities but, unlike the typical Sagittarian, you back up your words with some quite practical actions. People learn to trust you and the amount of reliance that is placed on your judgement is sometimes staggering. Of course this does infer a high degree of responsibility but this fact probably won't worry you in the slightest. From a personal point of view you are very good to know and do your best to be friendly to almost everyone. However, you don't suffer fools at all gladly and probably prefer the company of those whose thoughts and ideas run along the same sort of road as yours.

Nobody could dispute the fact that you are very reasonable but you do sometimes get so obsessed with things that you could be less accessible than Sagittarius. A little extra work may be needed in this direction, especially when you are dealing with people who don't have your fast-track approach to problems. For all this you are a deep thinker and will often weigh up the pros and cons of a particular problem if necessary. In love you are deep and sincere, but with a superficial veneer that makes you appear light, bright and fun to be with. Making your way in life isn't at all difficult and money could easily come your way. This is not a response to good luck, but to dedication and inspired hard work.

With a good combination of the practical and the inspirational, you could turn your hand to almost anything. Your confidence is usually high and you are always in a good position to get by, no matter what obstacles you encounter. You like a challenge and rarely shy away from things when the going gets tough. This is one of the reasons that others like you so much and also explains why they have such confidence in your abilities. Your sense of purpose is strong and you may be tougher than you realise.

The Aquarius Cusp – January 18th to 20th

This is the more dreamy side of Capricorn and can make for an individual who is sometimes rather difficult for others to fathom. This is hardly surprising since you don't really know your own nature quite as well as you would wish. Because the two zodiac signs are a little like oil and water you can rub along quite nicely for ages as a typical Capricorn, before suddenly shooting off at a tangent into some nether world that isn't at all like the reliable sign of the Goat. You tend to think about things fairly deeply, though with a rather 'off the wall' approach that sometimes annoys your deeper Capricorn traits. Certainly you are fascinating to know, with a magnetic personality and a basic charm that shows itself a great deal, especially when your interest is roused.

You are a lover of mystery and might appear on occasion to have a slightly dark side. This is really only a sort of morbid curiosity and it doesn't reflect your own basic nature, which is kind, sincere and anxious to please. Socially you contribute to anything that takes your fancy but you won't stay around long if you find a conversation boring. Finding the right sort of romantic partner might be somewhat difficult because you are not run-of-the-mill and have strange needs at a personal level. However, once you have set your sights in a particular direction, you stick to it. And as far as finding the right person is concerned, you could do much worse than to trust your intuition, which is strong. You don't always know what you want from life, but this fact can prove to be half of the fascination.

This unusual nature tends to fit you for occupations that demand a variety of skills, though you may change your career entirely at some stage in your life. Certainly you can be very practical, but the way things feel is important to you and you might find that you start certain tasks time and again in order to make sure that they turn out just right. This sign combination can easily lead to a desire for travel and a need to extend your personal horizons. Your restlessness is sometimes a puzzle to others, but it's a fascination, too.

CAPRICORN AND ITS ASCENDANTS

The nature of every individual on the planet is composed of the rich variety of zodiac signs and planetary positions that were present at the time of their birth. Your Sun sign, which in your case is Capricorn, is one of the many factors when it comes to assessing the unique person you are. Probably the most important consideration, other than your Sun sign, is to establish the zodiac sign that was rising over the eastern horizon at the time that you were born. This is your Ascending or Rising sign. Most popular astrology fails to take account of the Ascendant, and yet its importance remains with you from the very moment of your birth, through every day of your life. The Ascendant is evident in the way you approach the world, and so, when meeting a person for the first time, it is this astrological influence that you are most likely to notice first. Our Ascending sign essentially represents what we appear to be, while the Sun sign is what we feel inside ourselves.

The Ascendant also has the potential for modifying our overall nature. For example, if you were born at a time of day when Capricorn was passing over the eastern horizon (this would be around the time of dawn) then you would be classed as a double Capricorn. As such, you would typify this zodiac sign, both internally and in your dealings with others. However, if your Ascendant sign turned out to be an Air sign, such as Gemini, there would be a profound alteration of nature, away from the expected qualities of Capricorn.

One of the reasons why popular astrology often ignores the Ascendant is that it has always been rather difficult to establish. Old Moore has found a way to make this possible by devising an easy-to-use table, which you will find on page 125 of this book. Using this, you can establish your Ascendant sign at a glance. You will need to know your rough time of birth, then it is simply a case of following the instructions.

For those readers who have no idea of their time of birth it might be worth allowing a good friend, or perhaps your partner, to read through the section that follows this introduction. Someone who deals with you on a regular basis may easily discover your Ascending sign, even though you could have some difficulty establishing it for yourself. A good understanding of this component of your nature is essential if you want to be aware of that 'other person' who is responsible for the way you make contact with the world at large. Your Sun sign, Ascendant sign, and the other pointers in this book will, together, allow you a far better understanding of what makes you tick as an individual. Peeling back the different layers of your astrological make-up can be an enlightening experience, and the Ascendant may represent one of the most important layers of all.

Capricorn with Capricorn Ascendant

Whatever it is that you are looking for in life, there isn't much doubt that you find it. Having done so, you tend to consolidate your position before looking ahead to the next set of objectives. There isn't a more determined soul than you in the length and breadth of the whole zodiac and you will not be thwarted once you have made up your mind. It would take an astute person to pull the wool over your eyes in any practical respect, though you may not be quite so clever when it comes to the personal side of your life. You can sometimes be rather misled in love, but not if you are as determined in this direction as you are in every other sphere of life.

The most enduring quality that you possess is staying-power, and you remain certain that your long-term plans are the right ones, modifying here and tweaking there to get them just right. On the way you make few deep friends, though the ones you do have tend to stay around for years. All the same you are popular, and can attract the right sort of people to help you out. In love you are sincere and honest, a good and reliable partner, and, I am told, one of the best lovers to be found in a month of Sundays. All you need to complete the picture is a more flexible attitude.

Capricorn with Aquarius Ascendant

Here the determination of Capricorn is assisted by a slightly more adaptable quality and an off-beat personality that tends to keep everyone else guessing. You don't care to be quite so predictable as the archetypal Capricorn would be and there is a more idealistic quality, or at least one that shows more. A greater number of friends than Capricorn would usually keep is likely, though less than a true Aquarian would gather. Few people doubt your sincerity, though not all of them understand what makes you tick. Unfortunately you are not in a position to help them out, because you are not very sure yourself. All the same you muddle through and can be very capable when the mood takes you.

Being a natural traveller, you love to see new places and would be quite fascinated by cultures that are very different to your own. People with this combination are inclined to spend some time living abroad and may even settle there. You look out for the underdog and will always have time for a good cause, no matter what it takes to help. In romantic terms you are a reliable partner, though with a slightly wayward edge which, if anything, tends to make you more attractive. Listen to your intuition, which rarely lets you down. Generally speaking you are very popular.

Capricorn with Pisces Ascendant

You are certainly not the easiest person in the world to understand, mainly because your nature is so deep and your personality so complicated, that others are somewhat intimidated at the prospect of staring into this abyss. All the same your friendly nature is attractive, and there will always be people around who are fascinated by the sheer magnetic quality that is endemic to the zodiac mix. Sentimental and extremely kind, there is no limit to the extent of your efforts on behalf of a deserving world, though there are some people around who wonder at your commitment and who may ridicule you a little for your staying-power, even in the face of some adversity. At work you are very capable, will work long and hard, and can definitely expect a greater degree of financial and practical success than Pisces alone. Routines don't bother you too much, though you do need regular periods of introspection, which help to recharge low batteries and a battered self-esteem.

In affairs of the heart you are somewhat given to impulse, which belies the more careful qualities of Capricorn. However, the determination remains intact and you are quite capable of chasing rainbows around, never realising that you can't get to the end of them. You are immensely lovable and a great favourite to many.

Capricorn with Aries Ascendant

If ever anyone could be accused of setting off immediately, but slowly, it has to be you. These are very contradictory signs and the differences will express themselves in a variety of ways. One thing is certain, you have tremendous tenacity and will see a job through patiently from beginning to end, without tiring on the way, and ensuring that every detail is taken care of properly. This combination often bestows good health and a great capacity for continuity, particularly in terms of the length of life. You are certainly not as argumentative as the typical Aries, but you do know how to get your own way, which is just as well because you are usually thinking on behalf of everyone else and not just on your own account.

At home you can relax, which is a blessing for Aries, though in fact you seldom choose to do so because you always have some project or other on the go. You probably enjoy knocking down and rebuilding walls, though this is a practical tendency and not responsive to relationships, in which you are ardent and sincere. Impetuosity is as close to your heart as is the case for any type of Aries subject, though you certainly have the ability to appear patient and steady. But it's really just a front, isn't it?

Capricorn with Taurus Ascendant

It might appear on the surface that you are not the most interesting person in the world. This is a pity, for you have an active though very logical mind, so logical in some instances that you would have a great deal in common with Mr Spock. This is the thorn in your flesh, or rather the flesh of everyone else, since you are probably quite happy being exactly what you are. You can think things through in a clear and very practical way and end up taking decisions that are balanced, eminently sensible, but, on occasions, rather dull.

Actually there is a fun machine somewhere deep within that Earth-sign nature and those who know you the best will recognise the fact. Often this combination is attended by a deep and biting sense of humour, but it's of the sort that less intelligent and considered types would find rather difficult to recognise. It is likely that you have no lack of confidence in your own judgement, and you have all the attributes necessary to do very well on the financial front. Slow and steady progress is your way and you need to be quite certain before you commit yourself to any new venture. This is a zodiac combination that can soak up years of stress and numerous difficulties and yet still come out on top. Nothing holds you back for long and you tend to be very brave.

Capricorn with Gemini Ascendant

A very careful and considered combination is evident here. You still have the friendly and chatty qualities of Gemini, though you also possess an astute, clever and deep-thinking quality which can really add bite to the Mercurial aspects of your nature. Although you rarely seem to take yourself or anyone else too seriously, in reality you are not easily fooled and usually know the direction in which you are heading. The practical application of your thought processes matter to you and you always give of your best, especially in any professional situation. This combination provides the very best business mind that any Gemini could have and, unlike other versions of the sign, you are willing to allow matters to mature. This quality cannot be overstated and leads to a form of ultimate achievement that many other Geminis would only guess at.

Family matters are important to you and your home is a special place of retreat, even though you are also willing to get out and meet the world, which is the prerogative of all Gemini types. There are times when you genuinely wish to remain quiet, and when such times arise you may need to explain the situation to some of the bemused people surrounding you. Above all you look towards material gain, though without ever losing your sense of humour.

Capricorn with Cancer Ascendant

The single most important factor here is the practical ability to get things done and to see any task, professional or personal, through to the end. Since half this combination is Cancer that also means expounding much of your energy on behalf of others. There isn't a charity in the world that would fail to recognise what a potent combination this is when it comes to the very concrete side of offering help and assistance. Many of your ideas hold water and you don't set off on abortive journeys of any kind, simply because you tend to get the ground rules fixed in your mind first.

On a more personal level you can be rather hard to get to know, because both these signs have a deep quality and a tendency to keep things in the dark. The mystery may only serve to encourage people to try and get to know you better. As a result you could attract a host of admirers, many of whom would wish to form romantic attachments. This may prove to be irrelevant however, because once you give your heart, you tend to be loyal and would only change your mind if you were pushed into doing so. Prolonged periods of inactivity don't do you any good and it is sensible for you to keep on the move, even though your progress in life is measured and very steady.

Capricorn with Leo Ascendant

What really sets you apart is your endless patience and your determination to get where you want to go, no matter how long it takes you to do so. On the way there are many sub-plots in your life and a wealth of entertaining situations to keep you amused. Probably somewhat quieter than the average Leo, you still have the capacity to be the life and soul of the party on those occasions when it suits you to be so. Energy, when allied to persistence, is a powerful commodity and you have a great need to take on causes of one sort or another. Probably at your best when defending the rights of the oppressed, you take the protecting qualities of Leo to greater heights than almost anyone else touched by the idealistic and regal qualities of the sign. If arguments come into your life, you deal with them quickly and, in the main, wisely. Like most Capricorn types you take to a few individuals, who will play a part in your life for years on end.

Being a good family type, your partner and children are very important and you will lavish the same patience, determination and ultimate success on their behalf that you do when dealing with more remote situations. The fact is that you do not know any other way to behave, and you are at your best when there is a mountain to climb.

Capricorn with Virgo Ascendant

Your endurance, persistence and concentration are legendary, and there is virtually nothing that eludes you once you have the bit between your teeth. You are not the pushy, fussy, go-getting sort of Virgoan but are steady, methodical and very careful. Once you have made up your mind, a whole team of wild horses could not change it, and although this can be a distinct blessing at times, it is a quality that can bring odd problems into your life too. The difficulty starts when you adopt a lost or less than sensible cause. Even in the face of overwhelming negative evidence, there is something inside you that prevents any sort of U-turn and so you carry on as solidly as only you can, to a destination that won't suit you at all.

There are few people around who are more loyal and constant than you can be. There is a lighter and brighter side to your nature, and the one or two people who are most important in your life will know how to bring it out. You have a wicked sense of humour, particularly if you have had a drink or when you are feeling on top form. Travel does you the world of good, even if there is a part of you that would rather stay at home. You have a potent, powerful and magnetic personality, but for much of the time it is kept carefully hidden.

Capricorn with Libra Ascendant

It is a fact that Libra is the most patient of the Air signs, though like the others it needs to get things done fairly quickly. Capricorn, on the other hand, will work long and hard to achieve its objectives and will not be thwarted. As a result this is a powerful combination and one that leads ultimately to success.

Capricorn is often accused of taking itself too seriously, and yet it has an ironic and really very funny sense of humour which only its chief confidants recognise. Libra is lighthearted, always willing to have fun and quite anxious to please. When these two basic types come together in their best forms, you might find yourself to be one of the most well-balanced people around. Certainly you know what you want, but don't have to use a bulldozer in order to get it.

Active and enthusiastic when something really takes your fancy, you might also turn out to be one of the very best lovers of them all. The reason for this is that you have the depth of Capricorn but the lighter and more directly affectionate qualities of the Scales. What you want from life in a personal sense, you eventually tend to get, but you don't care too much if this takes you a while. Few people could deny that you are a faithful friend, a happy sort and a deeply magnetic personality.

Capricorn with Scorpio Ascendant

If patience, perseverance and a solid ability to get where you want to go are considered to be the chief components of a happy life, then you should be skipping about every day. Unfortunately this is not always the case, and here we have two zodiac signs who can both be too deep for their own good. Both Scorpio and Capricorn are inclined to take themselves rather too seriously, and your main lesson in life, and some would say the reason you have adopted this zodiac combination, is to 'lighten up'. If all that determination is pushed in the direction of your service to the world at large, you are seen as being one of the kindest people imaginable. This is really the only option for you, because if you turn this tremendous potential power inwards all the time you will become brooding, secretive and sometimes even selfish. Your eyes should be turned towards a needy humanity, which can be served with the dry but definite wit of Capricorn and the true compassion of Scorpio.

It is impossible with this combination to indicate what areas of life suit you the best. Certainly you adore luxury in all its forms, and yet you can get by with almost nothing. You desire travel, and at the same time love the comforts and stability of home. The people who know you best are aware that you are rather special. Listen to what they say.

Capricorn with Sagittarius Ascendant

The typical Sagittarian nature is modified for the better when Capricorn is part of the deal. It's true that you manage to push forward progressively under most circumstances, but you also possess staying power and can work long and hard to achieve your objectives, most of which are carefully planned in advance. Few people have the true measure of your nature, for it runs rather deeper than appears to be the case on the surface. Routines don't bother you as much as would be the case for Sagittarius when taken alone, and you don't care if any objective takes weeks, months or even years to achieve. You are very fond of those you take to and would certainly prove to be a capable friend, even when things get quite tough.

In love relationships you are steadfast and reliable, and yet you never lose the ability to entertain. Yours is a dry sense of humour which shows itself to a multitude of different people and which doesn't run out, even on those occasions when life gets tough. It might take you a long time to find the love of your life, but when you do there is a greater possibility of retaining the relationship for a long period. You don't tend to inherit money, but you can easily make it for yourself, though you won't worry too much about the amount. On the whole you are a very self-sufficient and sensible individual.

THE MOON AND THE PART IT PLAYS IN YOUR LIFE

In astrology the Moon is probably the single most important heavenly body after the Sun. Its unique position, as partner to the Earth on its journey around the solar system, means that the Moon appears to pass through the signs of the zodiac extremely quickly. The zodiac position of the Moon at the time of your birth plays a great part in personal character and is especially significant in the build-up of your emotional nature.

Sun Moon Cycles

The first lunar cycle deals with the part the position of the Moon plays relative to your Sun sign. I have made the fluctuations of this pattern easy for you to understand by means of a simple cyclic graph. It appears on the first page of each 'Your Month At A Glance', under the title 'Highs and Lows'. The graph displays the lunar cycle and you will soon learn to understand how its movements have a bearing on your level of energy and your abilities.

Your Own Moon Sign

Discovering the position of the Moon at the time of your birth has always been notoriously difficult because tracking the complex zodiac positions of the Moon is not easy. This process has been reduced to three simple stages with Old Moore's unique Lunar Tables. A breakdown of the Moon's zodiac positions can be found from page 28 onwards, so that once you know what your Moon Sign is, you can see what part this plays in the overall build-up of your personal character.

If you follow the instructions on the next page you will soon be able to work out exactly what zodiac sign the Moon occupied on the day that you were born and you can then go on to compare the reading for this position with those of your Sun sign and your Ascendant. It is partly the comparison between these three important positions that goes towards making you the unique individual you are.

HOW TO DISCOVER YOUR MOON SIGN

This is a three-stage process. You may need a pen and a piece of paper but if you follow the instructions below the process should only take a minute or so.

STAGE 1 First of all you need to know the Moon Age at the time of your birth. If you look at Moon Table 1, on page 26, you will find all the years between 1920 and 2018 down the left side. Find the year of your birth and then trace across to the right to the month of your birth. Where the two intersect you will find a number. This is the date of the New Moon in the month that you were born. You now need to count forward the number of days between the New Moon and your own birthday. For example, if the New Moon in the month of your birth was shown as being the 6th and you were born on the 20th, your Moon Age Day would be 14. If the New Moon in the month of your birth came after your birthday, you need to count forward from the New Moon in the previous month. If you were born in a Leap Year, remember to count the 29th February. You can tell if your birth year was a Leap Year if the last two digits can be divided by four. Whatever the result, jot this number down so that you do not forget it.

STAGE 2 Take a look at Moon Table 2 on page 27. Down the left hand column look for the date of your birth. Now trace across to the month of your birth. Where the two meet you will find a letter. Copy this letter down alongside your Moon Age Day.

STAGE 3 Moon Table 3 on page 27 will supply you with the zodiac sign the Moon occupied on the day of your birth. Look for your Moon Age Day down the left hand column and then for the letter you found in Stage 2. Where the two converge you will find a zodiac sign and this is the sign occupied by the Moon on the day that you were born.

Your Zodiac Moon Sign Explained

You will find a profile of all zodiac Moon Signs on pages 28 to 31, showing in yet another way how astrology helps to make you into the individual that you are. In each daily entry of the Astral Diary you can find the zodiac position of the Moon for every day of the year. This also allows you to discover your lunar birthdays. Since the Moon passes through all the signs of the zodiac in about a month, you can expect something like twelve lunar birthdays each year. At these times you are likely to be emotionally steady and able to make the sort of decisions that have real, lasting value.

Moon Table 1

YEAR	NOV	DEC	JAN	YEAR	NOV	DEC	JAN	YEAR	NOV	DEC	JAN
1920	10	10	20	1953	6	6	15	1986	2	1/30	10
1921	29	29	9	1954	25	25	5	1987	21	20	29
1922	19	18	27	1955	14	14	24	1988	9	9	19
1923	8	8	17	1956	2	2	13	1989	28	28	7
1924	26	26	6	1957	21	21	1/30	1990	17	17	26
1925	16	15	24	1958	11	10	19	1991	6	6	15
1926	5	5	14	1959	30	29	9	1992	24	24	4
1927	24	24	3	1960	19	18	27	1993	14	14	22
1928	12	12	21	1961	8	7	16	1994	3	2	11
1929	1	1/30	11	1962	27	26	6	1995	22	22	1
1930	20	19	29	1963	15	15	25	1996	11	10	20
1931	9	9	18	1964	4	4	14	1997	30	29	9
1932	27	27	7	1965	22	22	3	1998	19	18	28
1933	17	17	25	1966	12	12	21	1999	8	7	17
1934	7	6	15	1967	2	1/30	10	2000	27	25	6
1935	26	25	5	1968	21	20	29	2001	16	15	24
1936	14	13	24	1969	9	9	19	2002	4	4	13
1937	3	2	12	1970	29	28	7	2003	24	23	3
1938	22	21	1/31	1971	18	17	26	2004	11	11	21
1939	11	10	20	1972	6	6	15	2005	1	1	10
1940	29	28	9	1973	25	25	5	2006	20	20	29
1941	19	18	27	1974	14	14	24	2007	9	9	18
1942	8	8	16	1975	3	3	12	2008	28	27	8
1943	27	27	6	1976	21	21	1/31	2009	17	16	26
1944	15	15	25	1977	11	10	19	2010	6	6	15
1945	4	4	14	1978	30	29	9	2011	25	25	4
1946	23	23	3	1979	19	18	27	2012	13	12	23
1947	12	12	21	1980	8	7	16	2013	2	2	12
1948	1	1/30	11	1981	26	26	6	2014	22	22	1/31
1949	20	19	29	1982	15	15	25	2015	11	20	19
1950	9	9	18	1983	4	4	14	2016	29	29	9
1951	29	28	7	1984	22	22	3	2017	18	18	27
1952	17	17	26	1985	12	12	21	2018	07	07	16

Moon Tables 2 and 3

Table 2

DAY	DEC	JAN
1	i	A
2	i	A
3	m	A
4	m	A
5	n	A
6	n	A
7	n	A
8	n	A
9	n	A
10	n	A
11	n	B
12	n	B
13	n	B
14	n	B
15	n	B
16	n	B
17	n	B
18	n	B
19	n	B
20	n	B
21	n	C
22	n	C
23	q	C
24	q	C
25	q	C
26	q	C
27	q	C
28	q	C
29	q	C
30	q	C
31	q	C

Table 3

M/D	i	m	n	q	A	B	C
0	SA	SA	SA	CP	CP	AQ	AQ
1	SA	SA	CP	CP	AQ	AQ	AQ
2	CP	CP	CP	AQ	AQ	AQ	PI
3	CP	CP	AQ	AQ	AQ	PI	PI
4	CP	AQ	AQ	PI	PI	PI	AR
5	AQ	AQ	PI	PI	PI	AR	AR
6	AQ	AQ	PI	AR	AR	AR	AR
7	PI	PI	AR	AR	AR	AR	TA
8	PI	PI	AR	AR	AR	TA	TA
9	AR	AR	TA	TA	TA	TA	GE
10	AR	AR	TA	TA	TA	GE	GE
11	TA	TA	TA	GE	GE	GE	GE
12	TA	TA	GE	GE	GE	GE	CA
13	GE	GE	GE	GE	GE	CA	CA
14	GE	GE	CA	CA	CA	CA	LE
15	GE	GE	GE	CA	CA	LE	LE
16	GE	CA	CA	CA	LE	LE	LE
17	CA	CA	CA	LE	LE	LE	VI
18	CA	CA	LE	LE	LE	VI	VI
19	CA	LE	LE	LE	VI	VI	VI
20	LE	LE	LE	VI	VI	LI	LI
21	LE	LE	VI	VI	LI	LI	LI
22	VI	VI	VI	LI	LI	LI	SC
23	VI	VI	VI	LI	LI	SC	SC
24	VI	VI	LI	LI	SC	SC	SC
25	LI	LI	LI	SC	SC	SA	SA
26	LI	LI	SC	SC	SA	SA	SA
27	SC	SC	SC	SA	SA	SA	CP
28	SC	SC	SC	SA	SA	CP	CP
29	SC	SA	SA	SA	CP	CP	CP

AR = Aries, TA = Taurus, GE = Gemini, CA = Cancer, LE = Leo, VI = Virgo, LI = Libra, SC = Scorpio, SA = Sagittarius, CP = Capricorn, AQ = Aquarius, PI = Pisces

MOON SIGNS

Moon in Aries

You have a strong imagination, courage, determination and a desire to do things in your own way and forge your own path through life.

Originality is a key attribute; you are seldom stuck for ideas although your mind is changeable and you could take the time to focus on individual tasks. Often quick-tempered, you take orders from few people and live life at a fast pace. Avoid health problems by taking regular time out for rest and relaxation.

Emotionally, it is important that you talk to those you are closest to and work out your true feelings. Once you discover that people are there to help, there is less necessity for you to do everything yourself.

Moon in Taurus

The Moon in Taurus gives you a courteous and friendly manner, which means you are likely to have many friends.

The good things in life mean a lot to you, as Taurus is an Earth sign that delights in experiences which please the senses. Hence you are probably a lover of good food and drink, which may in turn mean you need to keep an eye on the bathroom scales, especially as looking good is also important to you.

Emotionally you are fairly stable and you stick by your own standards. Taureans do not respond well to change. Intuition also plays an important part in your life.

Moon in Gemini

You have a warm-hearted character, sympathetic and eager to help others. At times reserved, you can also be articulate and chatty: this is part of the paradox of Gemini, which always brings duplicity to the nature. You are interested in current affairs, have a good intellect, and are good company and likely to have many friends. Most of your friends have a high opinion of you and would be ready to defend you should the need arise. However, this is usually unnecessary, as you are quite capable of defending yourself in any verbal confrontation.

Travel is important to your inquisitive mind and you find intellectual stimulus in mixing with people from different cultures. You also gain much from reading, writing and the arts but you do need plenty of rest and relaxation in order to avoid fatigue.

Moon in Cancer

The Moon in Cancer at the time of birth is a fortunate position as Cancer is the Moon's natural home. This means that the qualities of compassion and understanding given by the Moon are especially enhanced in your nature, and you are friendly and sociable and cope well with emotional pressures. You cherish home and family life, and happily do the domestic tasks. Your surroundings are important to you and you hate squalor and filth. You are likely to have a love of music and poetry.

Your basic character, although at times changeable like the Moon itself, depends on symmetry. You aim to make your surroundings comfortable and harmonious, for yourself and those close to you.

Moon in Leo

The best qualities of the Moon and Leo come together to make you warmhearted, fair, ambitious and self-confident. With good organisational abilities, you invariably rise to a position of responsibility in your chosen career. This is fortunate as you don't enjoy being an 'also-ran' and would rather be an important part of a small organisation than a menial in a large one.

You should be lucky in love, and happy, provided you put in the effort to make a comfortable home for yourself and those close to you. It is likely that you will have a love of pleasure, sport, music and literature. Life brings you many rewards, most of them as a direct result of your own efforts, although you may be luckier than average and ready to make the best of any situation.

Moon in Virgo

You are endowed with good mental abilities and a keen receptive memory, but you are never ostentatious or pretentious. Naturally quite reserved, you still have many friends, especially of the opposite sex. Marital relationships must be discussed carefully and worked at so that they remain harmonious, as personal attachments can be a problem if you do not give them your full attention.

Talented and persevering, you possess artistic qualities and are a good homemaker. Earning your honours through genuine merit, you work long and hard towards your objectives but show little pride in your achievements. Many short journeys will be undertaken in your life.

Moon in Libra

With the Moon in Libra you are naturally popular and make friends easily. People like you, probably more than you realise, you bring fun to a party and are a natural diplomat. For all its good points, Libra is not the most stable of astrological signs and, as a result, your emotions can be a little unstable too. Therefore, although the Moon in Libra is said to be good for love and marriage, your Sun sign and Rising sign will have an important effect on your emotional and loving qualities.

You must remember to relate to others in your decision-making. Co-operation is crucial because Libra represents the 'balance' of life that can only be achieved through harmonious relationships. Conformity is not easy for you because Libra, an Air sign, likes its independence.

Moon in Scorpio

Some people might call you pushy. In fact, all you really want to do is to live life to the full and protect yourself and your family from the pressures of life. Take care to avoid giving the impression of being sarcastic or impulsive and use your energies wisely and constructively.

You have great courage and you invariably achieve your goals by force of personality and sheer effort. You are fond of mystery and are good at predicting the outcome of situations and events. Travel experiences can be beneficial to you.

You may experience problems if you do not take time to examine your motives in a relationship, and also if you allow jealousy, always a feature of Scorpio, to cloud your judgement.

Moon in Sagittarius

The Moon in Sagittarius helps to make you a generous individual with humanitarian qualities and a kind heart. Restlessness may be intrinsic as your mind is seldom still. Perhaps because of this, you have a need for change that could lead you to several major moves during your adult life. You are not afraid to stand your ground when you know your judgement is right, you speak directly and have good intuition.

At work you are quick, efficient and versatile and so you make an ideal employee. You need work to be intellectually demanding and do not enjoy tedious routines.

In relationships, you anger quickly if faced with stupidity or deception, though you are just as quick to forgive and forget. Emotionally, there are times when your heart rules your head.

Moon in Capricorn

The Moon in Capricorn makes you popular and likely to come into the public eye in some way. The watery Moon is not entirely comfortable in the Earth sign of Capricorn and this may lead to some difficulties in the early years of life. An initial lack of creative ability and indecision must be overcome before the true qualities of patience and perseverance inherent in Capricorn can show through.

You have good administrative ability and are a capable worker, and if you are careful you can accumulate wealth. But you must be cautious and take professional advice in partnerships, as you are open to deception. You may be interested in social or welfare work, which suit your organisational skills and sympathy for others.

Moon in Aquarius

The Moon in Aquarius makes you an active and agreeable person with a friendly, easy-going nature. Sympathetic to the needs of others, you flourish in a laid-back atmosphere. You are broad-minded, fair and open to suggestion, although sometimes you have an unconventional quality which others can find hard to understand.

You are interested in the strange and curious, and in old articles and places. You enjoy trips to these places and gain much from them. Political, scientific and educational work interests you and you might choose a career in science or technology.

Money-wise, you make gains through innovation and concentration and Lunar Aquarians often tackle more than one job at a time. In love you are kind and honest.

Moon in Pisces

You have a kind, sympathetic nature, somewhat retiring at times, but you always take account of others' feelings and help when you can.

Personal relationships may be problematic, but as life goes on you can learn from your experiences and develop a better understanding of yourself and the world around you.

You have a fondness for travel, appreciate beauty and harmony and hate disorder and strife. You may be fond of literature and would make a good writer or speaker yourself. You have a creative imagination and may come across as an incurable romantic. You have strong intuition, maybe bordering on a mediumistic quality, which sets you apart from the mass. You may not be rich in cash terms, but your personal gifts are worth more than gold.

CAPRICORN IN LOVE

Discover how compatible in love you are with people from the same and other signs of the zodiac. Five stars equals a match made in heaven!

Capricorn meets Capricorn

One of the best combinations because Capricorn knows what it wants and likes its partner to be the same. This may not be the deepest or most passionate of relationships, but Capricorn is adaptable enough to accept that. Material success is likely for this couple as they share the ability to move slowly towards even distant horizons. There will be words of love and a generally happy family atmosphere, and although at times the relationship may look lukewarm, it will usually remain strong and secure. Star rating: *****

Capricorn meets Aquarius

Probably one of the least likely combinations as Capricorn and Aquarius are unlikely to choose each other in the first place, unless one side is quite untypical of their sign. Capricorn approaches things in a practical way and likes to get things done, while Aquarius works almost exclusively for the moment and relies heavily on intuition. Their attitudes to romance are also diametrically opposed: Aquarius' moods tend to swing from red hot to ice cold in a minute, which is alien to steady Capricorn. Star rating: **

Capricorn meets Pisces

There is some chance of a happy relationship here, but it will need work on both sides. Capricorn is a go-getter, but likes to plan long term. Pisces is naturally more immediate, but has enough intuition to understand the Goat's thinking. Both have patience, but it will usually be Pisces who chooses to play second fiddle. The quiet nature of both signs might be a problem, as someone will have to lead, especially in social situations. Both signs should recognise this fact and accommodate it. Star rating: ***

Capricorn meets Aries

Capricorn works conscientiously to achieve its objectives and so can be the perfect companion for Aries. The Ram knows how to achieve but not how to consolidate, so the two signs have a great deal to offer one another practically. There may not be fireworks and it's sometimes doubtful how well they know each other, but it may not matter. Aries is outwardly hot but inwardly cool, whilst Capricorn can appear low-key but be a furnace underneath. Such a pairing can gradually find contentment, though both parties may wonder how this is so. Star rating: ****

Capricorn meets Taurus

If not quite a match made in heaven, this comes close. Both signs are Earthy in nature and that is a promising start. Capricorn is very practical and can make a Taurean's dreams come true. Both are tidy, like to know what is going to happen in a day-to-day sense, and are steady and committed. Taurus loves refinement, which Capricorn accepts and even helps to create. A good prognosis for material success rounds off a relationship that could easily stay the course. The only thing missing is a genuine sense of humour. Star rating: *****

Capricorn meets Gemini

Gemini has a natural fondness for Capricorn, which at first may be mutual. However, Capricorn is very organised, practical and persevering, and always achieves its goals in the end. Gemini starts out like this, but then starts to use a more instinctive and evolutionary approach, which may interfere with mutual objectives. To compensate, Gemini helps Capricorn avoid taking itself too seriously, while Capricorn brings a degree of stability into Gemini's world. When this pairing does work, though, it will be spectacular! Star rating: ***

Capricorn meets Cancer

Just about the only thing this pair have in common is the fact that both signs begin 'Ca'! Some signs of the zodiac are instigators and some are reactors, and both the Crab and the Goat are reactors. Consequently, they both need incentives from their partners but won't find it in each other and, with neither side taking the initiative, there's a spark missing. Cancer and Capricorn do think alike in some ways and so, if they can find their common purpose, they can be as happy as anyone. It's just rather unlikely. Star rating: **

Capricorn meets Leo

Despite promising appearances, this match often fails to take. Capricorn focuses on long-term objectives and, like Leo, is very practical. Both signs are capable of attaining success after a struggle, which, while requiring effort, gives them a mutual goal. But when life is easier, the cracks begin to show. Capricorn can be too serious for Leo, and the couple share few ideals. Leo loves luxury, Capricorn seeks austerity. Leo is warm but Capricorn seems cold and wintry in comparison. Both have many good points, but they don't seem to fire each other off properly. Star rating: **

Capricorn meets Virgo

One of the best possible combinations, because Virgo and Capricorn have an instinctive understanding. Both signs know the value of dedicated hard work and apply it equally in a relationship and other areas of life. Two of the most practical signs, nothing is beyond their ken, even if to outsiders they appear rather sterile or lacking in 'oomph'. What matters most is that the individuals are happy and with so much in common, the likelihood of mutual material success, and a shared devotion to home and family, there isn't much doubt of that. Star rating: *****

Capricorn meets Libra

Libra and Capricorn rub each other up the wrong way because their attitudes to life are so different, and although both are capable of doing something about this, in reality they probably won't. Capricorn is steady, determined and solid, while Libra is bright but sometimes superficial and not entirely reliable. They usually lack the instant spark needed to get them together in the first place, so when it does happen it is often because one of the partners is not very typical of their sign. Star rating: **

Capricorn meets Scorpio

Lack of communication is the governing factor here. Neither of this pair are renowned communicators and both need a partner to draw out their full verbal potential. Consequently, Scorpio may find Capricorn cold and unapproachable while Capricorn could find Scorpio dark and brooding. Both are naturally tidy and would keep a pristine house but great effort and a mutual goal is needed on both sides to overcome the missing spark. A good match on the financial side, but probably not an earthshattering personal encounter. Star rating: **

Capricorn meets Sagittarius

Any real problem here will stem from a lack of understanding. Capricorn is very practical and needs to be constantly on the go – though in a fairly low-key sort of way. Sagittarius is busy too, though always in a panic and invariably behind its deadlines, which will annoy organised Capricorn. Sagittarius doesn't really have the depth of nature that best suits an Earth sign like Capricorn and its flirty nature could upset the sensitive Goat, but their lighter attitude could be cheering, too. Star rating: ***

VENUS: THE PLANET OF LOVE

If you look up at the sky around sunset or sunrise you will often see Venus in close attendance to the Sun. It is arguably one of the most beautiful sights of all and there is little wonder that historically it became associated with the goddess of love. But although Venus does play an important part in the way you view love and in the way others see you romantically, this is only one of the spheres of influence that it enjoys in your overall character.

Venus has a part to play in the more cultured side of your life and has much to do with your appreciation of art, literature, music and general creativity. Even the way you look is responsive to the part of the zodiac that Venus occupied at the start of your life, though this fact is also down to your Sun sign and Ascending sign. If, at the time you were born, Venus occupied one of the more gregarious zodiac signs, you will be more likely to wear your heart on your sleeve, as well as to be more attracted to entertainment, social gatherings and good company. If on the other hand Venus occupied a quiet zodiac sign at the time of your birth, you would tend to be more retiring and less willing to shine in public situations.

It's good to know what part the planet Venus plays in your life, for it can have a great bearing on the way you appear to the rest of the world and since we all have to mix with others, you can learn to make the very best of what Venus has to offer you.

One of the great complications in the past has always been trying to establish exactly what zodiac position Venus enjoyed when you were born, because the planet is notoriously difficult to track. However, I have solved that problem by creating a table that is exclusive to your Sun sign, which you will find on the following page.

To calculate your Venus sign, first look up the year of your birth in the table. As Capricorn naturally spans two calendar years every time it comes around, double-check that you are looking at the right line. The table is organised so that December is always the first month, so, for instance, if you were born in December 1940 or January 1941 you would look at the column for 1940–1, because the year on the calendar has changed while the zodiac is still in the sign of Capricorn. If you were born in January 1942 you would look at the column for 1941–2. Once you have the right column, you will see a sign of the zodiac next to the date. This was the sign that Venus occupied in that year. If Venus occupied more than one sign during the period, this is indicated by the date on which the sign changed and the name of the new sign. For instance, if you are looking at the years 1940–1, Venus was in Sagittarius until the 15th January, after which time it was in Capricorn. If you were born before 15th January your Venus sign is Sagittarius, if you were born on or after 15th January, your Venus sign is Capricorn. Once you have established the position of Venus at the time of your birth, you can then look in the pages which follow to see how this has a bearing on your life.

Venus: The Planet of Love

1920–1	AQUARIUS / 7.1 PISCES	1969–70	SAGITTARIUS / 27.12 CAPRICORN
1921–2	SAGITTARIUS / 30.12 CAPRICORN	1970–1	SCORPIO / 5.1 SAGITTARIUS
1922–3	SCORPIO / 6.1 SAGITTARIUS	1971–2	CAPRICORN / 23.12 AQUARIUS / 16.1 PISCES
1923–4	CAPRICORN / 26.12 AQUARIUS / 19.1 PISCES	1972–3	SAGITTARIUS / 12.1 CAPRICORN
1924–5	SAGITTARIUS / 15.1 CAPRICORN	1973–4	AQUARIUS
1925–6	AQUARIUS	1974–5	CAPRICORN / 6.1 AQUARIUS
1926–7	CAPRICORN / 9.1 AQUARIUS	1975–6	SCORPIO / 1.1 SAGITTARIUS
1927–8	SCORPIO / 4.1 SAGITTARIUS	1976–7	AQUARIUS / 4.1 PISCES
1928–9	AQUARIUS / 6.1 PISCES	1977–8	SAGITTARIUS / 27.12 CAPRICORN
1929–30	SAGITTARIUS / 29.12 CAPRICORN	1978–9	SCORPIO / 5.1 SAGITTARIUS
1930–1	SCORPIO / 3.1 SAGITTARIUS	1979–80	CAPRICORN / 23.12 AQUARIUS / 16.1 PISCES
1931–2	CAPRICORN / 26.12 AQUARIUS / 19.1 PISCES	1980–1	SAGITTARIUS / 12.1 CAPRICORN
1932–3	SAGITTARIUS / 15.1 PISCES	1981–2	AQUARIUS
1933–4	AQUARIUS	1982–3	CAPRICORN / 6.1 AQUARIUS
1934–5	CAPRICORN / 9.1 AQUARIUS	1983–4	SCORPIO / 1.1 SAGITTARIUS
1935–6	SCORPIO / 4.1 SAGITTARIUS	1984–5	AQUARIUS / 4.1 PISCES
1936–7	AQUARIUS / 6.1 PISCES	1985–6	SAGITTARIUS / 27.12 CAPRICORN
1937–8	SAGITTARIUS / 29.12 CAPRICORN	1986–7	SCORPIO / 6.1 SAGITTARIUS
1938–9	SCORPIO / 3.1 SAGITTARIUS	1987–8	AQUARIUS / 15.1 PISCES
1939–40	CAPRICORN / 25.12 AQUARIUS / 18.1 PISCES	1988–9	SAGITTARIUS / 11.1 CAPRICORN
1940–1	SAGITTARIUS / 15.1 CAPRICORN	1989–90	AQUARIUS / 17.1 CAPRICORN
1941–2	AQUARIUS	1990–1	CAPRICORN / 5.1 AQUARIUS
1942–3	CAPRICORN / 8.1 AQUARIUS	1991–2	SCORPIO / 1.1 SAGITTARIUS
1943–4	SCORPIO / 3.1 SAGITTARIUS	1992–3	AQUARIUS / 4.1 PISCES
1944–5	AQUARIUS / 5.1 PISCES	1993–4	SAGITTARIUS / 26.12 CAPRICORN
1945–6	SAGITTARIUS / 28.12 CAPRICORN	1994–5	SCORPIO / 7.1 SAGITTARIUS
1946–7	SCORPIO / 3.1 SAGITTARIUS	1995–6	AQUARIUS / 15.1 PISCES
1947–8	CAPRICORN / 25.12 AQUARIUS / 18.1 PISCES	1996–7	SAGITTARIUS / 11.1 CAPRICORN
1948–9	SAGITTARIUS /14.1 CAPRICORN	1997–8	AQUARIUS / 14.1 CAPRICORN
1949–50	AQUARIUS	1998–9	CAPRICORN / 5.1 AQUARIUS
1950–1	CAPRICORN / 8.1 AQUARIUS	1999–00	SCORPIO / 1.1 SAGITTARIUS
1951–2	SCORPIO / 3.1 SAGITTARIUS	2000–01	SAGITTARIUS / 26.12 CAPRICORN
1952–3	AQUARIUS / 5.1 PISCES	2001–02	CAPRICORN / 4.1 AQUARIUS
1953–4	SAGITTARIUS / 28.12 CAPRICORN	2002–03	SAGITTARIUS / 26.12 CAPRICORN
1954–5	SCORPIO / 4.1 SAGITTARIUS	2003–04	SCORPIO / 7.1 SAGITTARIUS
1955–6	CAPRICORN / 24.12 AQUARIUS / 17.1 PISCES	2004–05	SAGITTARIUS / 30.12 CAPRICORN
1956–7	SAGITTARIUS / 14.1 CAPRICORN	2006–07	AQUARIUS / 14.1 CAPRICORN
1957–8	AQUARIUS	2007–08	CAPRICORN / 5.1 AQUARIUS
1958–9	CAPRICORN / 7.1 AQUARIUS	2008–09	SCORPIO / 1.1 SAGITTARIUS
1959–60	SCORPIO / 2.1 SAGITTARIUS	2009–10	SAGITTARIUS / 26.12 CAPRICORN
1960–1	AQUARIUS / 5.1 PISCES	2010–11	SAGITTARIUS / 26.12 CAPRICORN
1961–2	SAGITTARIUS / 1962–3 SCORPIO / 4.1 SAGITTARIUS	2011–12	CAPRICORN / 4.12 AQUARIUS
		2012–13	AQUARIUS / 14.1 CAPRICORN
1963–4	CAPRICORN / 24.12 AQUARIUS / 17.1 PISCES	2013–14	CAPRICORN / 5.1 AQUARIUS
1964–5	SAGITTARIUS / 13.1 CAPRICORN	2014–15	AQUARIUS / 14.1 CAPRICORN
1965–6	AQUARIUS	2015–16	CAPRICORN / 5.1 AQUARIUS
1966–7	CAPRICORN / 7.1 AQUARIUS	2016–17	AQUARIUS / 1.1 SAGITTARIUS
1967–8	SCORPIO / 2.1 SAGITTARIUS	2017–18	SAGITTARIUS / 26.12 CAPRICORN
1968–9	AQUARIUS / 5.1 PISCES	2018	SAGITTARIUS / 26.12 CAPRICORN

37

VENUS THROUGH THE ZODIAC SIGNS

Venus in Aries

Amongst other things, the position of Venus in Aries indicates a fondness for travel, music and all creative pursuits. Your nature tends to be affectionate and you would try not to create confusion or difficulty for others if it could be avoided. Many people with this planetary position have a great love of the theatre, and mental stimulation is of the greatest importance. Early romantic attachments are common with Venus in Aries, so it is very important to establish a genuine sense of romantic continuity. Early marriage is not recommended, especially if it is based on sympathy. You may give your heart a little too readily on occasions.

Venus in Taurus

You are capable of very deep feelings and your emotions tend to last for a very long time. This makes you a trusting partner and lover, whose constancy is second to none. In life you are precise and careful and always try to do things the right way. Although this means an ordered life, which you are comfortable with, it can also lead you to be rather too fussy for your own good. Despite your pleasant nature, you are very fixed in your opinions and quite able to speak your mind. Others are attracted to you and historical astrologers always quoted this position of Venus as being very fortunate in terms of marriage. However, if you find yourself involved in a failed relationship, it could take you a long time to trust again.

Venus in Gemini

As with all associations related to Gemini, you tend to be quite versatile, anxious for change and intelligent in your dealings with the world at large. You may gain money from more than one source but you are equally good at spending it. There is an inference here that you are a good communicator, via either the written or the spoken word, and you love to be in the company of interesting people. Always on the look-out for culture, you may also be very fond of music, and love to indulge the curious and cultured side of your nature. In romance you tend to have more than one relationship and could find yourself associated with someone who has previously been a friend or even a distant relative.

Venus in Cancer

You often stay close to home because you are very fond of family and enjoy many of your most treasured moments when you are with those you love. Being naturally sympathetic, you will always do anything you can to support those around you, even people you hardly know at all. This charitable side of your nature is your most noticeable trait and is one of the reasons why others are naturally so fond of you. Being receptive and in some cases even psychic, you can see through to the soul of most of those with whom you come into contact. You may not commence too many romantic attachments but when you do give your heart, it tends to be unconditionally.

Venus in Leo

It must become quickly obvious to almost anyone you meet that you are kind, sympathetic and yet determined enough to stand up for anyone or anything that is truly important to you. Bright and sunny, you warm the world with your natural enthusiasm and would rarely do anything to hurt those around you, or at least not intentionally. In romance you are ardent and sincere, though some may find your style just a little overpowering. Gains come through your contacts with other people and this could be especially true with regard to romance, for love and money often come hand in hand for those who were born with Venus in Leo. People claim to understand you, though you are more complex than you seem.

Venus in Virgo

Your nature could well be fairly quiet no matter what your Sun sign might be, though this fact often manifests itself as an inner peace and would not prevent you from being basically sociable. Some delays and even the odd disappointment in love cannot be ruled out with this planetary position, though it's a fact that you will usually find the happiness you look for in the end. Catapulting yourself into romantic entanglements that you know to be rather ill-advised is not sensible, and it would be better to wait before you committed yourself exclusively to any one person. It is the essence of your nature to serve the world at large and through doing so it is possible that you will attract money at some stage in your life.

Venus in Libra

Venus is very comfortable in Libra and bestows upon those people who have this planetary position a particular sort of kindness that is easy to recognise. This is a very good position for all sorts of friendships and also for romantic attachments that usually bring much joy into your life. Few individuals with Venus in Libra would avoid marriage and since you are capable of great depths of love, it is likely that you will find a contented personal life. You like to mix with people of integrity and intelligence but don't take kindly to scruffy surroundings or work that means getting your hands too dirty. Careful speculation, good business dealings and money through marriage all seem fairly likely.

Venus in Scorpio

You are quite open and tend to spend money quite freely, even on those occasions when you don't have very much. Although your intentions are always good, there are times when you get yourself in to the odd scrape and this can be particularly true when it comes to romance, which you may come to late or from a rather unexpected direction. Certainly you have the power to be happy and to make others contented on the way, but you find the odd stumbling block on your journey through life and it could seem that you have to work harder than those around you. As a result of this, you gain a much deeper understanding of the true value of personal happiness than many people ever do, and are likely to achieve true contentment in the end.

Venus in Sagittarius

You are lighthearted, cheerful and always able to see the funny side of any situation. These facts enhance your popularity, which is especially high with members of the opposite sex. You should never have to look too far to find romantic interest in your life, though it is just possible that you might be too willing to commit yourself before you are certain that the person in question is right for you. Part of the problem here extends to other areas of life too. The fact is that you like variety in everything and so can tire of situations that fail to offer it. All the same, if you choose wisely and learn to understand your restless side, then great happiness can be yours.

Venus in Capricorn

The most notable trait that comes from Venus in this position is that it makes you trustworthy and able to take on all sorts of responsibilities in life. People are instinctively fond of you and love you all the more because you are always ready to help those who are in any form of need. Social and business popularity can be yours and there is a magnetic quality to your nature that is particularly attractive in a romantic sense. Anyone who wants a partner for a lover, a spouse and a good friend too would almost certainly look in your direction. Constancy is the hallmark of your nature and unfaithfulness would go right against the grain. You might sometimes be a little too trusting.

Venus in Aquarius

This location of Venus offers a fondness for travel and a desire to try out something new at every possible opportunity. You are extremely easy to get along with and tend to have many friends from varied backgrounds, classes and inclinations. You like to live a distinct sort of life and gain a great deal from moving about, both in a career sense and with regard to your home. It is not out of the question that you could form a romantic attachment to someone who comes from far away or be attracted to a person of a distinctly artistic and original nature. What you cannot stand is jealousy, for you have friends of both sexes and would want to keep things that way.

Venus in Pisces

The first thing people tend to notice about you is your wonderful, warm smile. Being very charitable by nature you will do anything to help others, even if you don't know them well. Much of your life may be spent sorting out situations for other people, but it is very important to feel that you are living for yourself too. In the main, you remain cheerful, and tend to be quite attractive to members of the opposite sex. Where romantic attachments are concerned, you could be drawn to people who are significantly older or younger than yourself or to someone with a unique career or point of view. It might be best for you to avoid marrying whilst you are still very young.

HOW THE DIAGRAMS WORK

Through the picture diagrams in the Astral Diary I want to help you to plot your year. With them you can see where the positive and negative aspects will be found in each month. To make the most of them, all you have to do is remember where and when!

Let me show you how they work ...

THE MONTH AT A GLANCE

Just as there are twelve separate zodiac signs, so astrologers believe that each sign has twelve separate aspects to life. Each of the twelve segments relates to a different personal aspect. I list them all every month so that their meanings are always clear.

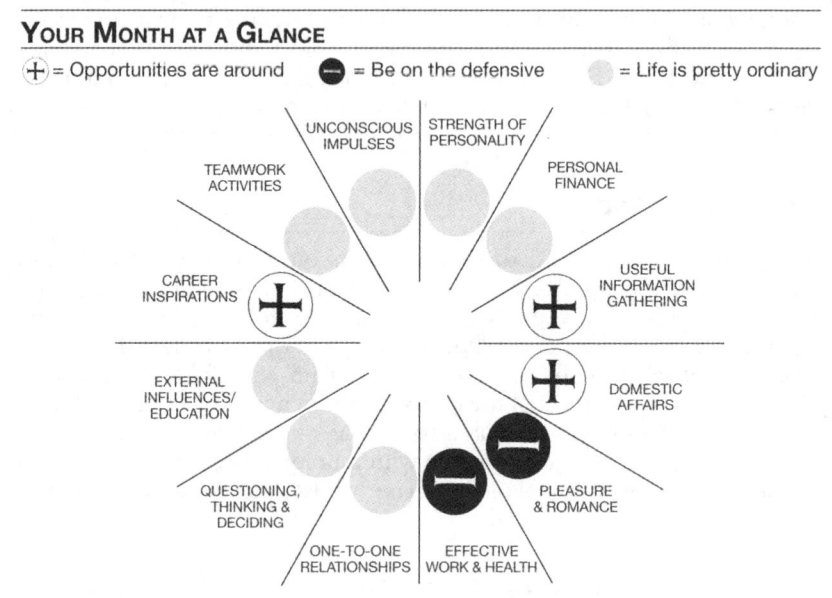

YOUR MONTH AT A GLANCE

⊕ = Opportunities are around   ⊖ = Be on the defensive   ● = Life is pretty ordinary

- UNCONSCIOUS IMPULSES
- STRENGTH OF PERSONALITY
- TEAMWORK ACTIVITIES
- PERSONAL FINANCE
- CAREER INSPIRATIONS
- USEFUL INFORMATION GATHERING
- EXTERNAL INFLUENCES/ EDUCATION
- DOMESTIC AFFAIRS
- QUESTIONING, THINKING & DECIDING
- PLEASURE & ROMANCE
- ONE-TO-ONE RELATIONSHIPS
- EFFECTIVE WORK & HEALTH

I have designed this chart to show you how and when these twelve different aspects are being influenced throughout the year. When there is a shaded circle, nothing out of the ordinary is to be expected. However, when a circle turns white with a plus sign, the influence is positive. Where the circle is black with a minus sign, it is a negative.

How the Diagrams Work

YOUR ENERGY RHYTHM CHART

Below is a picture diagram in which I link your zodiac group to the rhythm of the Moon. In doing this I have calculated when you will be gaining strength from its influence and equally when you may be weakened by it.

If you think of yourself as being like the tides of the ocean then you may understand how your own energies must also rise and fall. And if you understand how it works and when it is working, then you can better organise your activities to achieve more and get things done more easily.

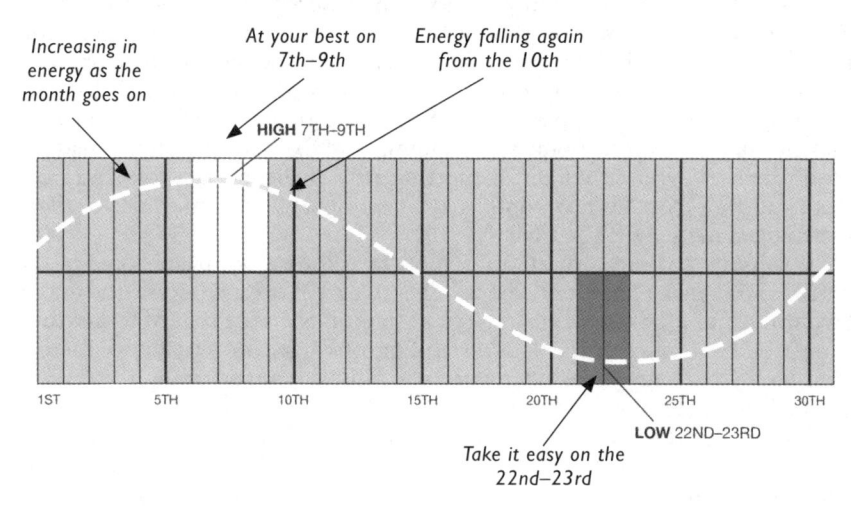

Increasing in energy as the month goes on

At your best on 7th–9th

Energy falling again from the 10th

HIGH 7TH–9TH

1ST   5TH   10TH   15TH   20TH   25TH   30TH

LOW 22ND–23RD

Take it easy on the 22nd–23rd

THE KEY DAYS

Some of the entries are in **bold**, which indicates the working of astrological cycles in your life. Look out for them each week as they are the best days to take action or make decisions. The daily text tells you which area of your life to focus on.

MERCURY RETROGRADE

The Mercury symbol (☿) indicates that Mercury is retrograde on that day. Since Mercury governs communication, the fact that it appears to be moving backwards when viewed from the Earth at this time should warn you that your communication skills are not likely to be at their best and you could expect some setbacks.

43

CAPRICORN: YOUR YEAR IN BRIEF

There is little doubt that this is a year during which you need to start as you mean to go on and not allow the negative thoughts of others to have a bearing on your own life. January and February offer all the incentive you need to get ahead at work and you should be especially well motivated at this time. Money matters may be variable but planning for the short and medium-term is definitely to be recommended. Keep a realistic sense of proportion.

With March and April comes the spring and this adds a little extra incentive to your efforts, particularly in a domestic sense. This is a time for making changes to your home surroundings and for resolving family matters. Don't be slow when it comes to meeting new challenges at work head on. April can be especially rewarding in a financial sense and may also see you sweeping someone off their feet.

It is likely that the early summer months will turn out to be some of the best for you in an all-round sense. This is partly because good fortune is favouring your efforts to a greater extent but it is also true that May and June bring you to a much firmer understanding of what you actually want from your life. Others might consider you to be quite enigmatic though, so expect to need to explain yourself frequently.

July and August look potentially lucky in a financial sense but much depends on the way you approach things. You will need a confident attitude and once you have made up your mind about anything you should stick to it. You may feel the need to travel and to spread your wings in all sorts of ways. A change of job, or the chance to take on new responsibilities at work is not out of the question.

As the summer comes to an end, September and October see you making ever-greater steps forward in a personal and a romantic sense, even if practical matters are now a little more difficult to address. Lean on the help and support provided by other people. October in particular should bring something very special in terms of either a new relationship or a rejuvenation of a present one.

November and December might at first sight seem the least helpful months for you because a number of obstacles are being put in your path. However, it is with the resolution of these that you come to a much better understanding of yourself and of life. The Christmas period should be packed with possibilities and may not turn out at all the way you expected. Finish the year with a flourish and in possession of some definite optimism for the future.

January 2018

Your Month at a Glance

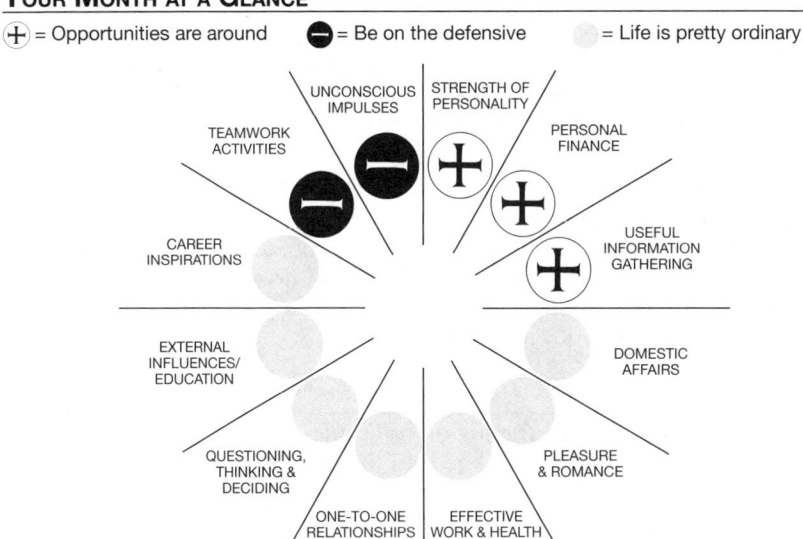

⊕ = Opportunities are around   ⊖ = Be on the defensive   ○ = Life is pretty ordinary

- TEAMWORK ACTIVITIES
- UNCONSCIOUS IMPULSES ⊖
- STRENGTH OF PERSONALITY ⊖
- PERSONAL FINANCE ⊕
- USEFUL INFORMATION GATHERING ⊕
- CAREER INSPIRATIONS
- EXTERNAL INFLUENCES/ EDUCATION
- DOMESTIC AFFAIRS
- QUESTIONING, THINKING & DECIDING
- PLEASURE & ROMANCE
- ONE-TO-ONE RELATIONSHIPS
- EFFECTIVE WORK & HEALTH

January Highs and Lows

Here I show you how the rhythms of the Moon will affect you this month. Like the tide, your energies and abilities will rise and fall with its pattern. When it is above the centre line, go for it, when it is below, you should be resting.

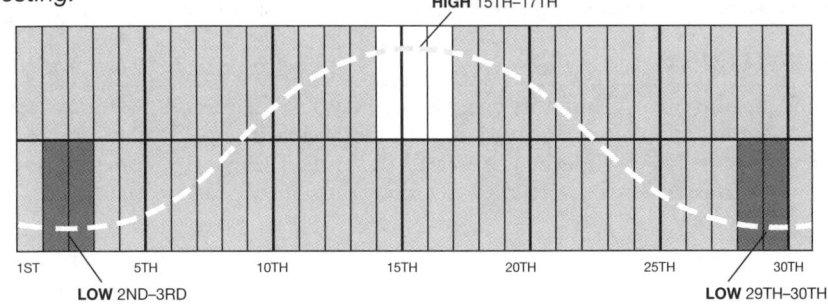

HIGH 15TH–17TH
LOW 2ND–3RD
LOW 29TH–30TH

45

Your Daily Guide to January 2018

1 MONDAY *Moon Age Day 14   Moon Sign Gemini*

For Capricorn the year could begin with a slightly unfortunate trend governing how you deal with others. It isn't that people are doing anything specifically designed to upset or frustrate you, but perhaps they don't get on with things in the way you would. Leave people to be who they are, while you pursue your own objectives the way you wish.

2 TUESDAY *Moon Age Day 15   Moon Sign Cancer*

The Moon has now entered Cancer, which is your opposite zodiac sign. This brings with it the lunar low, a monthly happening that tends to slow you down and to cause you to be more introspective than usual. You don't lack invitations or incentive – it is simply that you don't feel like exerting yourself.

3 WEDNESDAY *Moon Age Day 16   Moon Sign Cancer*

You are almost certainly going to be quiet today – not because you are particularly worried about anything but simply on account of the lunar low. Planning is now better than doing and you can do yourself a great deal of good by thinking about the future and comparing what lies ahead of you with examples of situations from the past.

4 THURSDAY *Moon Age Day 17   Moon Sign Leo*

Make yourself available to friends or colleagues who are going through a hard time. You can help lighten the load for them and your support will be much appreciated. It looks as though extra or different responsibility is about to come your way but you should be able to deal with this quite easily and even with significant optimism.

5 FRIDAY *Moon Age Day 18   Moon Sign Leo*

Expect some changes, especially at work. You don't always care for surprises, especially when they upset your routine but there are times when alterations are good for you, and if you don't bury your head in the sand they should not take you unawares. It's simply a matter of remaining open-minded.

6 SATURDAY *Moon Age Day 19   Moon Sign Virgo*

This may be one of the most energy-filled days so far this year. Things seem to come together to offer you a good time and you should be full of good ideas. Although you might not get all that much done in a concrete sense you will grasp every opportunity to enjoy yourself in good company.

7 SUNDAY
Moon Age Day 20   Moon Sign Virgo

Because this is a Sunday there is every chance that you can call at least part of today your own. You patiently persevere when you are doing things that appeal to you but you may not be exhibiting a sparkling personality. This is because there are things on your mind that are occupying your thoughts.

8 MONDAY
Moon Age Day 21   Moon Sign Libra

It is important to Capricorn to go about things in the right way, so you can sometimes get upset when people cut corners or cheat. Today you will be a role model to everyone around you. Awkward trends are out of the way and you should be feeling more energetic. People will relish having you around and listen to your advice.

9 TUESDAY
Moon Age Day 22   Moon Sign Libra

Be bold today, otherwise you might give the wrong impression to some fairly interesting people. Not everyone will agree with your point of view and you might find really unusual or radical points of view difficult to deal with. For your own part, though, you tend to be quite orthodox in your thinking.

10 WEDNESDAY
Moon Age Day 23   Moon Sign Scorpio

Events are starting to move along rapidly and you could have the feeling that some situations are running ahead of you. If this is the case you will probably panic and do everything you can to slow down the roller coaster of life. This is your way, although it might be quite stimulating to take your foot off the brakes and enjoy the thrill.

11 THURSDAY
Moon Age Day 24   Moon Sign Scorpio

Strongly perceptive, you could surprise others when your hunches pay off today. It is important to stick at a particular job today, though of course that isn't hard for Capricorn. If you find you can't sort something out, it might be necessary to swallow your pride and ask someone else for advice.

12 FRIDAY
Moon Age Day 25   Moon Sign Scorpio

Do your best to be different and original, especially in close relationships. Keep people guessing a little and flirt outrageously in social situations. This is all part of making people notice you because Capricorn can sometimes merge into the background. The last thing you want right now is to be sidelined in any way.

Your Daily Guide to January 2018

13 SATURDAY *Moon Age Day 26   Moon Sign Sagittarius*

People should be generally happy to go along with your plans, though for the moment you might feel that they know better. Avoid getting involved in family rows and, where possible, isolate yourself from difficult situations. By tomorrow you will be right on form but for today at least you are quieter and more reserved than usual.

14 SUNDAY *Moon Age Day 27   Moon Sign Sagittarius*

You seem to excel today at jobs those around you find difficult. Your powers of concentration are especially good and you will be very much in charge of anything that takes your fancy. Even when you are occupied with tasks you often find to be repetitive or boring you can find a way to make them enjoyable.

15 MONDAY *Moon Age Day 28   Moon Sign Capricorn*

Today things really begin to happen for you. The Moon has moved into your own zodiac sign of Capricorn, bringing that part of the month known as the lunar high. There is more incentive, greater reserves of energy and a stronger determination to get what you want from life. Your general level of good luck should also be higher now.

16 TUESDAY *Moon Age Day 0   Moon Sign Capricorn*

Keep up the pressure to get what you want. With everything to play for and people virtually tripping over themselves to lend you a hand you should be a winner all round. You could probably afford to take the odd chance today but you are unlikely to do so in terms of money because it isn't your way to take risks where cash is concerned.

17 WEDNESDAY *Moon Age Day 1   Moon Sign Capricorn*

The urge for freedom is paramount and you will fight hard against any sort of restriction. You will be all for personal rights under present planetary trends and won't be at all enamoured of a nanny state that seems to constantly tread on your toes. While well informed, Capricorn is also likely to be slightly outspoken.

18 THURSDAY *Moon Age Day 2   Moon Sign Aquarius*

Material issues and goals at work could get extra support at this stage of the week and speaking of goals, you will probably be far more sporting than usual at the moment. For once you are a team player, no matter what you happen to be doing. Getting on well with colleagues comes naturally now.

Your Daily Guide to January 2018

19 FRIDAY
Moon Age Day 3   Moon Sign Aquarius

Your spirits remain generally strong and you need to find more and more ways in which to show your creativity. This can be something as simple as making minor changes in and around your home but it could also extend to taking up new hobbies or pastimes that offer you much more self-expression than usual.

20 SATURDAY
Moon Age Day 4   Moon Sign Pisces

There may be a relationship or an intimate issue that requires attention so don't get so wrapped up in outside issues that you forget about your partner or close family members. People may have to remind you of your obligations, which is indeed rare in the life for Capricorn. It's just so easy to get sidetracked right now.

21 SUNDAY
Moon Age Day 5   Moon Sign Pisces

Work in progress seems to be especially rewarding now and you remain generally confident regarding your own thoughts and actions. The same may not be true with regard to colleagues or friends, some of whom are behaving in a rather strange manner. A few pointed questions may be the best way forward now.

22 MONDAY
Moon Age Day 6   Moon Sign Pisces

What really appeals to you at the moment is exchanging ideas and fact-finding. Just about anything can activate your grey cells and you show time and again just how bright you can be. You should also be turning to the written word in order to express yourself more fully with text messages and emails becoming ever more important.

23 TUESDAY
Moon Age Day 7   Moon Sign Aries

You invariably have a great talent for dealing with people and this shows strongly at the moment. Almost anyone who comes along holds some sort of fascination for you and it isn't hard under present trends for you to know instinctively what makes those around you tick. This is also a fine time to express your emotions in terms of love.

24 WEDNESDAY
Moon Age Day 8   Moon Sign Aries

Right now you are looking for things to do that will utilise your general helpfulness and allow you to be as charitable as you would like. You will want to go to any length to prove your love and to show your loyalty. Just don't put all that effort into a relationship that you know is already past its sell-by date.

25 THURSDAY
Moon Age Day 9   Moon Sign Taurus

You will positively insist on being number one today, which is great as far as you are concerned but can be quite tiresome to others. The fact is that you need to build your own self-confidence and you are likely to do this at the expense of others, so be aware that a little consideration for others may be necessary.

26 FRIDAY
Moon Age Day 10   Moon Sign Taurus

You will now do everything you can to ensure that things are going well in your working environment. This means not only knowing what is expected of you but also how other people have a bearing on situations. Listen to colleagues and do whatever you can to make their lot easier, as well as your own.

27 SATURDAY
Moon Age Day 11   Moon Sign Gemini

Routines will suit you much more than they do some of the people with whom you live and work. You like to know what is expected of you and it is no problem for you to do things time and again in the same way. Whilst they say variety is the spice of life, for Capricorn constancy is often more important.

28 SUNDAY
Moon Age Day 12   Moon Sign Gemini

The smooth running of your life could be thrown into turmoil today unless you guard what you have very carefully. This is certainly not the best time of the month to be spending lavishly or to take chances with relationships. Everything will be back to normal soon but right now things could look odd.

29 MONDAY
Moon Age Day 13   Moon Sign Cancer

You remain very sensitive to the impression you get from others. You will be listening very carefully to what people have to say and won't be at all inclined to push your luck or to go where you know you might feel insecure. This is the least positive side of Capricorn at work but in the main almost everything should be going your way.

30 TUESDAY
Moon Age Day 14   Moon Sign Cancer

Today you work well in any group environment and you will also revel in the chance to get out of the house and into new situations. The great outdoors may well appeal to you, even though winter winds could be blowing strongly. It is important at the moment that you can see wide horizons, both inside and outside your mind.

31 WEDNESDAY Moon Age Day 15 Moon Sign Leo

This should be a very pleasant time of the month when you are able to impress those around you. Maybe those in a position of authority are gazing in your direction and wondering what they can do to help you out? All in all, you have what it takes to get ahead and to make the best possible impression.

♑ February 2018

Your Month at a Glance

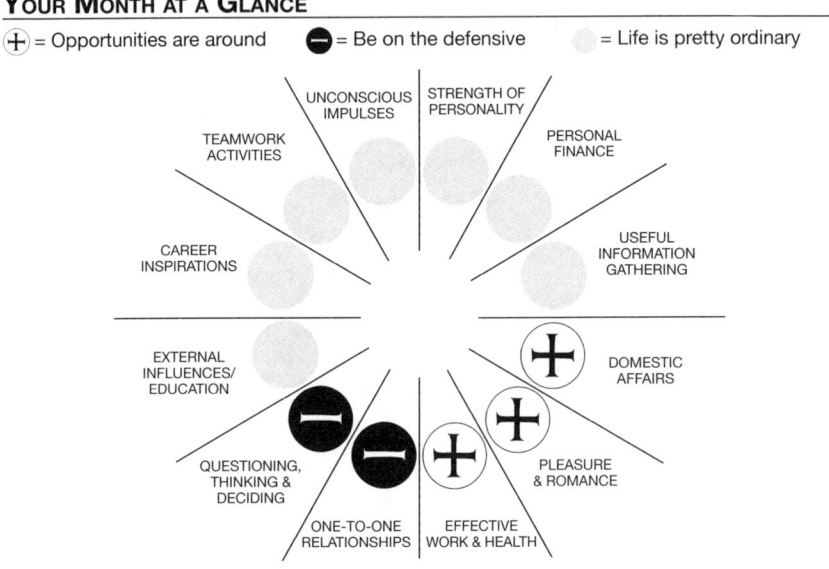

(+) = Opportunities are around   (−) = Be on the defensive   = Life is pretty ordinary

- UNCONSCIOUS IMPULSES
- STRENGTH OF PERSONALITY
- TEAMWORK ACTIVITIES
- PERSONAL FINANCE
- CAREER INSPIRATIONS
- USEFUL INFORMATION GATHERING
- EXTERNAL INFLUENCES/ EDUCATION
- DOMESTIC AFFAIRS (+)
- QUESTIONING, THINKING & DECIDING (−)
- PLEASURE & ROMANCE (+)
- ONE-TO-ONE RELATIONSHIPS (−)
- EFFECTIVE WORK & HEALTH (+)

February Highs and Lows

Here I show you how the rhythms of the Moon will affect you this month. Like the tide, your energies and abilities will rise and fall with its pattern. When it is above the centre line, go for it, when it is below, you should be resting.

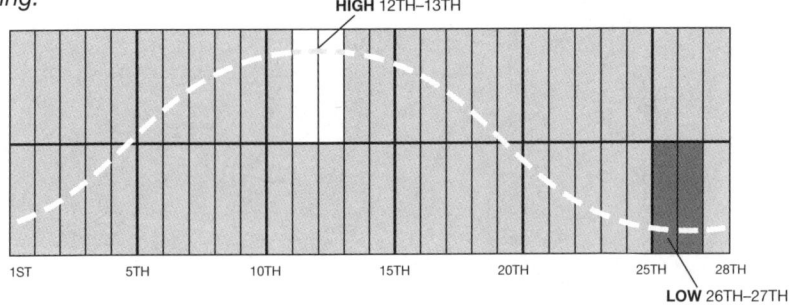

HIGH 12TH–13TH

1ST   5TH   10TH   15TH   20TH   25TH   28TH

LOW 26TH–27TH

52

Your Daily Guide to February 2018

1 THURSDAY *Moon Age Day 16   Moon Sign Leo*

The attitude of family members might take some working out. Make sure you haven't missed a significant date or anniversary, though it would be very unlike you to do so. It could just be that you are rubbing people up the wrong way and a change of approach may be called for. On the financial front things should be going well.

2 FRIDAY *Moon Age Day 17   Moon Sign Virgo*

If this is the last day of the working week for you it would be wise not to leave anything half finished. The best results around now come from completing one task before you begin another. This is the Capricorn way and brings the most satisfaction but there is a slight danger that you are presently inclined to take on too much.

3 SATURDAY *Moon Age Day 18   Moon Sign Virgo*

Trends influence your love life now, though the effect they have depends on your personal circumstances. Permanent attachments are likely to be strengthened, while Capricorns who are looking for love could well find it appearing in less than expected places. Home trends are good for all Capricorns today.

4 SUNDAY *Moon Age Day 19   Moon Sign Libra*

Finish the weekend with a flourish. Get involved in social activities and family events. Be willing to spend time outside of your home and even though the weather could be very wintry, get some fresh air and exercise. Your mind remains extremely active and in spare moments you may worry for no sensible reason.

5 MONDAY *Moon Age Day 20   Moon Sign Libra*

The response you get from others, especially colleagues, can be quite unexpected. You may have to think on your feet and there is just a slight possibility of disputes breaking out if people want to change your routines in any way. In a fussy mood, you won't take kindly to being manipulated or bamboozled.

6 TUESDAY *Moon Age Day 21   Moon Sign Libra*

Don't be surprised if you are on the receiving end of unexpected kindness today. This probably comes as a result of something you have done in the past and should be well deserved. You are now less fussy and willing to take on board new concepts. People will find you good to have around and the social invitations should be coming in.

7 WEDNESDAY
Moon Age Day 22 Moon Sign Scorpio

From a social point of view it appears that you are number one in the estimation of your friends. Keeping up with all that is on offer might be difficult and you will have to make some choices if you are not to overcrowd your schedule. To add to the possible confusion you may have to help out at home.

8 THURSDAY
Moon Age Day 23 Moon Sign Scorpio

You continue to be quick in your reasoning and inspirational in your thinking. While others are stuck in old ways you are (surprisingly for Capricorn) a creature of the moment. All this originality is inspiring and you will also be very good with words under present planetary trends. Not only can you do things, you can also talk about it.

9 FRIDAY
Moon Age Day 24 Moon Sign Sagittarius

You probably would not describe yourself as being particularly brave but others might. This is especially true when you are defending someone you think has been wronged and you could get very indignant on their behalf. Nothing is too much trouble for you when you are looking out for someone you care about.

10 SATURDAY
Moon Age Day 25 Moon Sign Sagittarius

Make this a different sort of day. Go on a shopping spree with a friend, get involved in a new sport or activity and keep your ears open when you are in company. It's amazing what you might hear at this time, and the most unlikely eventualities can start with a casual remark. Be bold when you are dealing with people in authority.

11 SUNDAY
Moon Age Day 26 Moon Sign Sagittarius

The more you push yourself, the greater the present rewards are likely to be. Don't be content with achieving one objective – get straight on to the next one. You could experience a degree of impatience if others fail to live up to your expectations but you are likely to cope with this in a good-humoured way.

12 MONDAY
Moon Age Day 27 Moon Sign Capricorn

It looks as though things couldn't be better as this week gets started. The lunar high gives you extra energy and the Moon in your own zodiac sign also makes you astute and quick to arrive at some important conclusions. It might be said that good fortune is on your side but in reality you are making your own luck today and tomorrow.

Your Daily Guide to February 2018

13 TUESDAY
Moon Age Day 28   Moon Sign Capricorn

The lunar high is still on your side and you should have all the incentive you need to make progress in any sphere of your life. There are new people around and a feeling that situations that have been difficult in the past are now going your way. You might also be making important new friends.

14 WEDNESDAY
Moon Age Day 29   Moon Sign Aquarius

Now you can reinforce recent efforts by putting the finishing touches to a particular task. This might come earlier than expected, probably because of the help you receive from others. Making up your mind to alter something at home could take time, but try to strike as quickly as possible while the iron is hot.

15 THURSDAY
Moon Age Day 0   Moon Sign Aquarius

What you learn from colleagues and friends today could be of the utmost importance to you. It is certainly worthwhile keeping your ears open, even when you are listening only to gossip. Intuition is high at the moment and you will almost instinctively make the right decision under most circumstances. Friends should prove to be loyal.

16 FRIDAY
Moon Age Day 1   Moon Sign Aquarius

Lots of drive will go into getting what you want at this stage of the week and your energy seems to be virtually boundless. Rewards could be generally greater than you expect, though one particular job, that seemed fairly straightforward, could turn out to be more complicated than you expected. Remain patient and plod on.

17 SATURDAY
Moon Age Day 2   Moon Sign Pisces

There is much that can be accomplished at this time. If you enjoy a challenge, now is the time to put yourself to the test. You can channel your energies down specific avenues and work as hard as ever towards your ultimate objectives. You might find there is help around from some surprising directions.

18 SUNDAY
Moon Age Day 3   Moon Sign Pisces

Seek out variety and if you are spending time with family members on this particular Sunday do something quite different that will inspire everyone. It might be difficult to get people moving, but you are good at prodding them into action. Once activity is underway, life begins to take on its own momentum.

19 MONDAY
Moon Age Day 4   Moon Sign Aries

You rely on your personal charm when it comes to getting more or less what you want from those around you. Even strangers will not be immune to your delightful nature at present and you are certainly likely to be less stubborn than is sometimes the case. Now is the time to ask others for things you really want.

20 TUESDAY
Moon Age Day 5   Moon Sign Aries

Social activities are fun and you won't be taking anything too seriously at this time. Do exert a little caution though, because some of the expectations you have regarding career matters could be rather too advanced for present circumstances. As always for you, patience is the key to greater achievement.

21 WEDNESDAY
Moon Age Day 6   Moon Sign Taurus

You should easily be able to find the support you need from others, especially in professional matters. Where attention to detail is required you will now be at your very best. Situations that require sound judgement and discrimination should go best of all. Others rely on you heavily for your skill in this.

22 THURSDAY
Moon Age Day 7   Moon Sign Taurus

This is one of the best times of the month for being the centre of attention. You should find this week to be really good in terms of social matters and you are likely to be giving the best impression of yourself all round. If there is one thing you do need to fight against it could be stubbornness at some stage.

23 FRIDAY
Moon Age Day 8   Moon Sign Taurus

Spend as much time as you can with loved ones and especially with your partner. Personal relationships should be working out very well for you and romance can play a significant part in your life between now and the weekend. Remain busy in a practical sense and you can get all sorts of jobs out of the way.

24 SATURDAY
Moon Age Day 9   Moon Sign Gemini

Your ability to impress others remains very strong, even though it might seem that not everyone is listening to you. That's why it is important to keep trying and not to allow doubts to creep into your mind. If you can be decisive, so much the better but it's far more likely that you will be moving forward quite cautiously on this Saturday.

25 SUNDAY
Moon Age Day 10   Moon Sign Gemini

Push on with your ambitions as if it is inevitable that they will turn out entirely the way you wish, and in all probability they will. With little room for doubt or hesitation, you can make progress if you are at work, and at the same time keep your relatives and friends happy. That way they will do anything for you.

26 MONDAY
Moon Age Day 11   Moon Sign Cancer

The Moon now enters your opposite zodiac sign of Cancer, which means the lunar low will be with you for a couple of days. You could notice that you are now more inclined to withdraw into your shell and you won't want to face up to some home truths. Treat the lunar low as a sort of holiday and avoid getting over stressed.

27 TUESDAY
Moon Age Day 12   Moon Sign Cancer

The more you relax, the less potent this period will be. There is plenty to be done but you won't feel like doing any of it. Keep on the move in a gentle sense and try to maintain a degree of variety in your life. Not everyone seems to be on your side at the moment but there is a possibility that you are misconstruing someone's motives.

28 WEDNESDAY
Moon Age Day 13   Moon Sign Leo

Taking chances will lead to excellent results, but if you worry yourself too much on the way they might not be worth what you have to go through. It might be best to settle for calculated risks, which are the sort you like best. Look out for people coming into your life who have something new and interesting to say.

March 2018

Your Month at a Glance

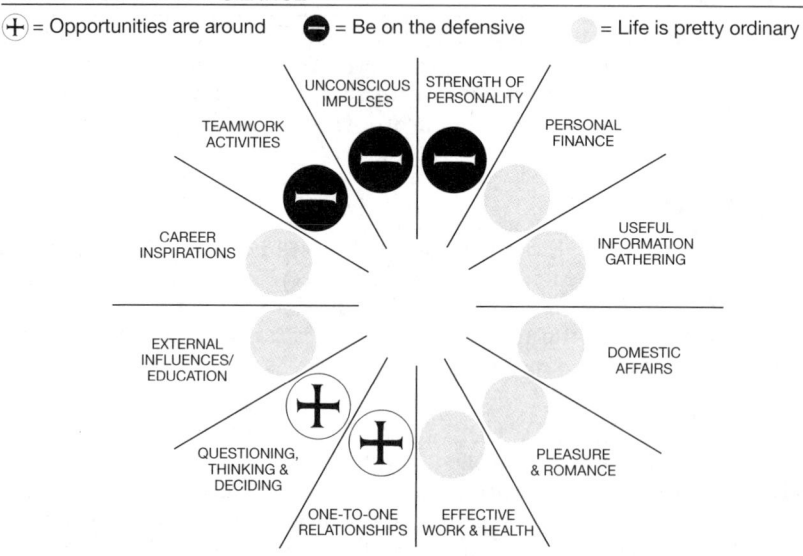

(+) = Opportunities are around ⊖ = Be on the defensive ◯ = Life is pretty ordinary

- UNCONSCIOUS IMPULSES: −
- STRENGTH OF PERSONALITY: −
- TEAMWORK ACTIVITIES: −
- PERSONAL FINANCE: ordinary
- CAREER INSPIRATIONS: ordinary
- USEFUL INFORMATION GATHERING: ordinary
- EXTERNAL INFLUENCES/EDUCATION: ordinary
- DOMESTIC AFFAIRS: ordinary
- QUESTIONING, THINKING & DECIDING: +
- PLEASURE & ROMANCE: ordinary
- ONE-TO-ONE RELATIONSHIPS: +
- EFFECTIVE WORK & HEALTH: ordinary

March Highs and Lows

Here I show you how the rhythms of the Moon will affect you this month. Like the tide, your energies and abilities will rise and fall with its pattern. When it is above the centre line, go for it, when it is below, you should be resting.

HIGH 11TH–12TH

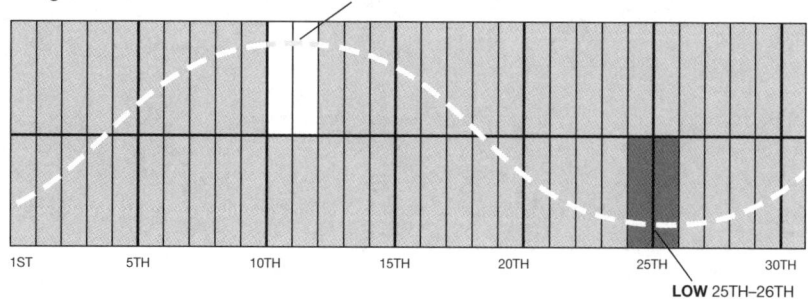

LOW 25TH–26TH

Your Daily Guide to March 2018

1 THURSDAY
Moon Age Day 14   Moon Sign Leo

When facing issues that have a bearing on your life at present you can draw on the most potent ally today. This is experience. Capricorn is like an elephant because it never forgets and you can a great deal of headway by basing your actions and reactions on what has gone before. This leads to a good chance of success.

2 FRIDAY
Moon Age Day 15   Moon Sign Virgo

Be bold in conversation and just slightly dominant in relationships. People will want you to take the lead and will be generally pleased to let you make the majority of decisions. Help is around when you need it but this tends to be advice rather than practical assistance. Listen to what younger family members are saying now.

3 SATURDAY
Moon Age Day 16   Moon Sign Virgo

It is important for you to create a stimulating atmosphere around yourself and your active mind is always on the go. With some very positive supporting influences surrounding you there is no reason to delay or to be in the background. People notice you a great deal at this time so put on a good show.

4 SUNDAY
Moon Age Day 17   Moon Sign Libra

You will find yourself amongst the right sort of company today and should discover that you have much in common with people who probably have not figured much in your life before. New romantic opportunities could be on the horizon and if you are in a settled relationship you should notice a greater warmth developing.

5 MONDAY
Moon Age Day 18   Moon Sign Libra

Your typical Capricorn qualities are now to the fore and you will especially like to be of service to others. Unfortunately you could also be rather too fussy for your own good and will want everything done your way. You will hate waste more than ever at the moment and you are likely to be very precise in the way you go about everything.

6 TUESDAY
Moon Age Day 19   Moon Sign Scorpio

People are likely to challenge your ideas today but that won't matter at all because you have exactly what it takes to counter their opposition. You might not find much support for your particular slant on life amongst colleagues but friends are more likely to form a receptive audience. Keep up with current affairs and local news today.

7 WEDNESDAY — Moon Age Day 20 — Moon Sign Scorpio

Today is favourable for close partnerships, aided by the present position of the planet Venus. However, this doesn't simply mean that romantic attachments will be on your mind because business attachments are also well highlighted. Any enduring contact with another person is worthy of note today.

8 THURSDAY — Moon Age Day 21 — Moon Sign Sagittarius

You have a strong desire for social contact right now and will be doing all you can to make new friends and to stimulate a positive response from the pals you already have. More willing than usual to act on impulse, there is a good chance you will score a few successes in terms of finances. Small gains are likely.

9 FRIDAY — Moon Age Day 22 — Moon Sign Sagittarius

Practical affairs could bring a sense of insecurity. You are not altogether sure that you have people in the right boxes so may be fishing in order to discover their point of view. In some ways this could put you on the defensive, especially when you are dealing with individuals who are as astute as you are.

10 SATURDAY — Moon Age Day 23 — Moon Sign Sagittarius

It is easy for you to work through anything you see as being superficial, though you should take care because amongst the dross is something that is more worthy of your attention. Keep up your efforts to get ahead financially, but don't spend money today in order to make more because trends indicate that it won't work.

11 SUNDAY — Moon Age Day 24 — Moon Sign Capricorn

If there is one thing that Capricorn could benefit from, it is variety. You don't always want it and if it means changing what you know and respect it can be very difficult. Today offers new starts, alternative ways of looking at old situations and brand new friends. What you make of all this remains to be seen but try to be open-minded.

12 MONDAY — Moon Age Day 25 — Moon Sign Capricorn

The lunar high continues to put you in situations that mean thinking on your feet. You could be surprised at your own ingenuity and most of the luck you experience today is made by you. It is truly amazing how much situations can change when you approach them with optimism. Love could come along at a moment's notice today.

Your Daily Guide to March 2018

13 TUESDAY
Moon Age Day 26   Moon Sign Aquarius

Relationships can be very intense and you may have to work hard in order to fully understand the way your partner is feeling at present. Not everyone is going to be on your side in a professional or a personal sense and some people may be trying to suggest you don't know what you are doing. Take all this with a pinch of salt.

14 WEDNESDAY
Moon Age Day 27   Moon Sign Aquarius

What a wonderful day this should be for conversation with anyone. You can learn so much by listening and, in turn, inspire people with your own experiences and point of view. You are quite gentle in your approach and people will genuinely want to have you around and to draw as much from you as they can.

15 THURSDAY
Moon Age Day 28   Moon Sign Aquarius

Problems will now lose some of their power to hold you back. You have been chipping away at a few minor difficulties and now everything will seem to line up at the same time to offer rewards. Significant gains can come along in terms of romance and if you have been making a play for a certain individual some success is likely.

16 FRIDAY
Moon Age Day 29   Moon Sign Pisces

If there is something you can jettison from your life, then so much the better. You are probably trying to walk too fast and do too much. Take a leaf out of the book of someone you really admire and also someone who has a great deal to teach you. You are not short of confidence, but don't rush all the same.

17 SATURDAY
Moon Age Day 0   Moon Sign Pisces

Relationships generally should be strong and even exciting today because people have things to tell you that will be right up your street. Offers today could lead to exciting opportunities in the future, as well as towards some fairly extraordinary situations that you could be facing almost immediately. Support long-standing friends if they need it.

18 SUNDAY
Moon Age Day 1   Moon Sign Aries

There are some people around who would do just about anything to get one over on you, probably because they know in their hearts they don't have your poise or talent. On the other side of the coin, some of the people you meet will find you both hypnotic and fascinating. Seek out the latter ones.

19 MONDAY　　　　　　　　　　　　　*Moon Age Day 2　Moon Sign Aries*

You have the secret of popularity worked out well at this time and you will be quite inclined to work this talent for all you are worth. Prepare for some fairly strange events and concentrate on what you are supposed to be doing without distractions. Get to grips with alterations you want to make at home.

20 TUESDAY　　　　　　　　　　　　　*Moon Age Day 3　Moon Sign Aries*

You may have a good insight into fundamental problems that surround you, even if you are not contributing to them in any way. You can't find exactly what you want coming from the direction of colleagues or friends and in many cases you will have to look for it within yourself. Think about starting a new book or doing a puzzle today.

21 WEDNESDAY　　　　　　　　　　　*Moon Age Day 4　Moon Sign Taurus*

Hidden tensions begin to bubble up and you could find a few people really difficult to deal with. Try to keep your patience and don't do anything to make a bad situation worse. Use a little ingenuity when it comes to your romantic needs and do whatever is necessary in order to sweep someone off their feet.

22 THURSDAY　　　　　　　　　　　　*Moon Age Day 5　Moon Sign Taurus*

You have good psychological insight and the ability to understand what makes others tick, even if these same individuals have been a mystery to you in the past. Record events today in as much detail as you can, even if it is only in terms of your thoughts. Gains can be made when it comes to making more money.

23 FRIDAY　　☿　　　　　　　　　　　*Moon Age Day 6　Moon Sign Gemini*

You really do need to get your act together today when it comes to your work. Capricorns who are between jobs at the moment should use the present trends to look around very carefully. Something is on offer, even if it seems unlikely at first. In almost all situations, Capricorn is its own best advocate now.

24 SATURDAY　　☿　　　　　　　　　*Moon Age Day 7　Moon Sign Gemini*

This is a great time for assessing what is important to you and for going out to get it. This being a Saturday, you may not be at work, but whether you are or not you can still make a good impression on most of the people you meet. Some very good ideas for making more money are on offer, so start talking to people about them.

♑ *Your Daily Guide to March 2018*

25 SUNDAY ☿ *Moon Age Day 8   Moon Sign Cancer*

False optimism is likely while the lunar low prevails and you could also be high-minded to the point of doing yourself no good at all. Try to be realistic and to accept the world the way it is – at least for the moment. Your chance to put things right will come but for the moment rest, relax and bide your time.

26 MONDAY ☿ *Moon Age Day 9   Moon Sign Cancer*

Avoid being party to any sort of deception. Be absolutely truthful whilst the lunar low is around, which fortunately is not difficult for Capricorn. If you do get embroiled in dubious situations you could be led into problems that will take ages to resolve. This is not a good day for signing important documents.

27 TUESDAY ☿ *Moon Age Day 10   Moon Sign Leo*

Now you enter a phase when you can formulate new goals in a very positive manner. Doing two things at once is part of what you are about and you will also be picking up a range of new skills. With a lot of good ideas, you don't waste anything today and may discover that you can utilise what others might refer to as rubbish.

28 WEDNESDAY ☿ *Moon Age Day 11   Moon Sign Leo*

A period of transformation is now in progress – one that might challenge you but which will also prove to be stimulating. There are some aspects of the past that you will have to let go of almost immediately – at least you will if you want to prosper from everything that is on offer under present planetary trends.

29 THURSDAY ☿ *Moon Age Day 12   Moon Sign Virgo*

If your major plans are flawed in any way, they won't work out as you would wish. There is all the more reason today to take advice and to explain yourself to others. Give people credit for knowing their own specialities best and watch what they are doing. Even the wisest person realises that there is always something new to learn.

30 FRIDAY ☿ *Moon Age Day 13   Moon Sign Virgo*

You may now have to consider whether or not you need certain things in life. Material considerations are not half as important today as the food you can find for your soul. This can be picked up in all your associations with others. In personal attachments you could be quite nostalgic and deeply romantic.

31 SATURDAY ☿   *Moon Age Day 14   Moon Sign Libra*

You have the capacity to take on diverse roles at the moment and you will be well able to accommodate a range of different sorts of personalities. You may meet some unusual people, some of whom hold views of which are very different from your own. Keep plugging away to find some common ground.

April 2018

Your Month at a Glance

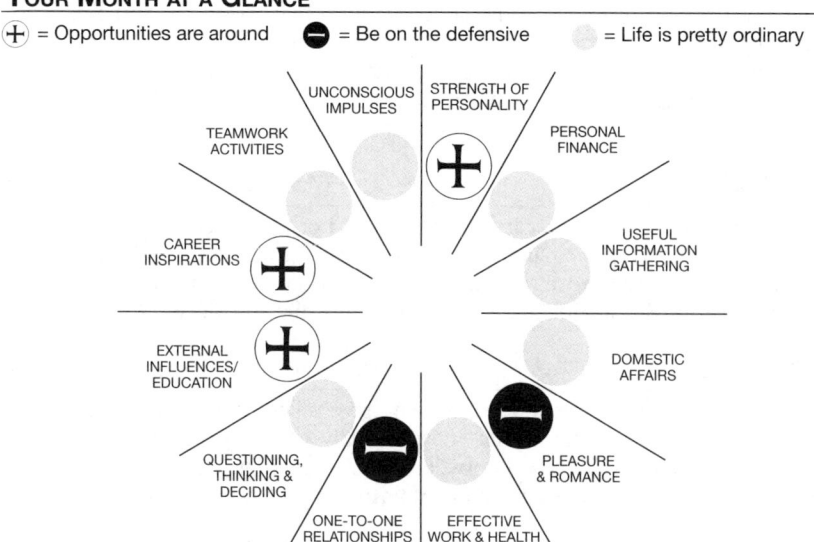

(+) = Opportunities are around   (−) = Be on the defensive   ○ = Life is pretty ordinary

- STRENGTH OF PERSONALITY: +
- CAREER INSPIRATIONS: +
- EXTERNAL INFLUENCES/EDUCATION: +
- UNCONSCIOUS IMPULSES: ordinary
- TEAMWORK ACTIVITIES: ordinary
- PERSONAL FINANCE: ordinary
- USEFUL INFORMATION GATHERING: ordinary
- DOMESTIC AFFAIRS: ordinary
- QUESTIONING, THINKING & DECIDING: −
- PLEASURE & ROMANCE: −
- ONE-TO-ONE RELATIONSHIPS: ordinary
- EFFECTIVE WORK & HEALTH: ordinary

April Highs and Lows

Here I show you how the rhythms of the Moon will affect you this month. Like the tide, your energies and abilities will rise and fall with its pattern. When it is above the centre line, go for it, when it is below, you should be resting.

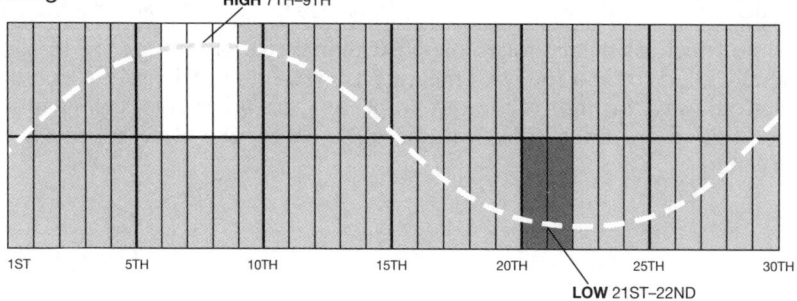

HIGH 7TH–9TH

LOW 21ST–22ND

65

1 SUNDAY ☿ *Moon Age Day 15   Moon Sign Libra*

Avoid unnecessary distractions and, whenever possible, stick to the matter at hand. This is April Fool's Day and you won't want to fall foul of anyone who thinks they can get one over on you. All the same if this does happen you will have to laugh it off and not get upset. Any embarrassment will soon pass.

2 MONDAY ☿ *Moon Age Day 16   Moon Sign Scorpio*

You may feel the need for some sort of renewal in your life and this week would be a good time to set it in motion. Mars helps you out and this alone can bring about significant change. Reorganisation at home would probably help but it is in the professional sphere that you are most likely to make alterations.

3 TUESDAY ☿ *Moon Age Day 17   Moon Sign Scorpio*

Now you could easily get carried away and perhaps even slightly deluded regarding your own personal goals. Some problems and responsibilities could be getting you down more than they usually would though this is really only a state of mind. Be optimistic, even if that feels difficult now.

4 WEDNESDAY ☿ *Moon Age Day 18   Moon Sign Scorpio*

A personal plan or a current scheme may have to be totally scrapped, or else modified to such an extent that it isn't really the same at all. This might disappoint you but you are happy enough with new starts once you get going. Expect to need patience to deal with people you find foolish now.

5 THURSDAY ☿ *Moon Age Day 19   Moon Sign Sagittarius*

Life should be fascinating today and trends suggest you might make some new friends. The more you commit yourself to outside influences the less you remain locked inside yourself. Search out some excitement when you are not working and avoid contemplation. Friends can be inspirational.

6 FRIDAY ☿ *Moon Age Day 20   Moon Sign Sagittarius*

With so much planetary focus on professional matters things are looking generally good for you today. Some aspects can seem restrictive but you can work your way through these and come out the other side feeling much more positive. Inspiring conversations are likely to take place, especially by the evening.

Your Daily Guide to April 2018

7 SATURDAY ☿ *Moon Age Day 21   Moon Sign Capricorn*

New initiatives and ideas are now resolving themselves in your mind and you are all activity and fun at this time. You could talk almost anyone into anything and it is not difficult for you to manipulate situations to your own ends. Not that you will be doing so selfishly. Right now you are as warm and caring as it is possible to be.

8 SUNDAY ☿ *Moon Age Day 22   Moon Sign Capricorn*

A plan that has been up in the air for quite some time is now likely to get the go-ahead and you are quite willing to put yourself out a great deal in order to achieve your longed-for objectives. At the same time you have good luck on your side and can impress the right people by talking and acting in the way Capricorn does when at its best.

9 MONDAY ☿ *Moon Age Day 23   Moon Sign Capricorn*

Along comes a lift to social matters and a greater commitment to group activities. You will become less inclined to spend time on your own and much more willing to join in with whatever is taking place around you. Friends will find you approachable and will want to involve you in whatever plans they have.

10 TUESDAY ☿ *Moon Age Day 24   Moon Sign Aquarius*

There is likely to be a more acquisitive side to your nature under present trends, though this isn't entirely surprising for Capricorn. Getting your own way won't be hard, especially in family situations but colleagues could be more difficult to deal with and will require a very sensitive approach. Friends need your active support right now.

11 WEDNESDAY ☿ *Moon Age Day 25   Moon Sign Aquarius*

You bring out the best in others, especially at work, and your psychological approach is now second-to-none. There is nothing brash about you but you will be cheerful and even exciting to have around. If ever there was a good time to mix business with pleasure this is it. New opportunities arise all the time.

12 THURSDAY ☿ *Moon Age Day 26   Moon Sign Pisces*

Your talent for creating and maintaining growth, allied to your ability when it comes to pleasing others makes for a formidable combination right now. This is especially useful to you if you are at work. Whatever else you are doing today take time out to praise younger family members.

13 FRIDAY ☿   Moon Age Day 27   Moon Sign Pisces

Today can be socially uplifting and brings a positive boost to all creative matters. You are romantically inclined and you know how to get the best from other people. Not that you are too obvious in your actions. There is a great subtlety about you now and you approach your objectives in a very sensitive manner.

14 SATURDAY ☿   Moon Age Day 28   Moon Sign Pisces

Personal success is not quite as important to you around the middle of this month as the happiness of those you love. Much of your time this weekend is likely to spent with family, especially your partner. Practical things suddenly don't seem important and you can take a holiday from responsibilities.

15 SUNDAY   Moon Age Day 29   Moon Sign Aries

Tension could now arise in partnerships, mainly because of your present changeability. You know what you want – the problem is that you don't really know how you can get it. This makes you seem dissatisfied when seen through the eyes of others. Seek their advice and they may learn to view you differently.

16 MONDAY   Moon Age Day 0   Moon Sign Aries

What you learn from colleagues or friends today might be both interesting and useful. At the same time use your creativity now and turn your amazing mind in the direction of issues that others find difficult to address. Keep up your efforts to make a good impression on someone you care for.

17 TUESDAY   Moon Age Day 1   Moon Sign Taurus

This is a day when you are both constructive and exciting to know. Professional developments could be on your mind and you move forward with much greater certainty than you may have done earlier in the year. It may dawn on you that you can do something you previously thought was impossible.

18 WEDNESDAY   Moon Age Day 2   Moon Sign Taurus

This ought to be an enjoyable and in some ways quite magical sort of day. Although there is great change taking place around you, there is also a deep and dreamy side to life that keeps you relaxed and calm. In some ways it's as if you are watching someone else's story, even though you are directly involved.

19 THURSDAY
Moon Age Day 3   Moon Sign Gemini

You could quite easily get caught up in disagreements today so avoid needless rows about issues that really are not too important in any case. Co-ordinate your efforts with others for the best chance of success at work, and as far as home-based projects are concerned, seek the opinions of family members now.

20 FRIDAY
Moon Age Day 4   Moon Sign Gemini

If you indulge in pleasures too much today, this could turn out to be quite an expensive time. Try to think a little before you part with cash, especially as, with a little extra planning, you could get some real bargains. This might mean having to wait a day or two but you will surely be pleased in the longer-term.

21 SATURDAY
Moon Age Day 5   Moon Sign Cancer

Keep a low profile at this time of the lunar low and try to leave others to take on the responsibility while you sit in a comfortable chair and supervise. You are not likely to isolate yourself in a physical sense, even though you are quite contemplative now. Mental puzzles would appeal to you.

22 SUNDAY
Moon Age Day 6   Moon Sign Cancer

You will still be generally cautious but the lunar low is a little different this month because it brings as many positives and negatives. You are likely to think deeply about certain issues and to reach conclusions that have escaped you in the past. You might also be quite magnetic in the eyes of would-be admirers.

23 MONDAY
Moon Age Day 7   Moon Sign Leo

Versatility is the key to success for Capricorn today. There's nothing new about that but you really are able to turn your versatility and your mind to almost anything. You could discover that you have a skill you never suspected and your hand-to-eye co-ordination is likely to be especially good. Make the most of little blessings by this evening.

24 TUESDAY
Moon Age Day 8   Moon Sign Leo

Family and domestic issues are on the up. Although you can be quite busy with practical jobs today, you also seem to be spending some significant time looking at relationships and the way you have been dealing with them. People generally are on your side and that makes the details of life easier to deal with.

25 WEDNESDAY
Moon Age Day 9   Moon Sign Virgo

You could attract a great deal of attention today and people will quite naturally want to know what you are doing. There is no end to your curiosity, which finds you turning over stones wherever you go. A trip away from home would suit you fine on this particular Wednesday, more so if the weather is good.

26 THURSDAY
Moon Age Day 10   Moon Sign Virgo

Today can be peaceful and secure on a material level but somewhat complicated as far as your personal life is concerned. It could be something as simple as having to reorganise your schedule to suit the needs of a family member or something much more demanding. Either way, you can deal with pressure very well today.

27 FRIDAY
Moon Age Day 11   Moon Sign Virgo

You can now become much more focused and may reserve your greatest curiosity for issues that normally wouldn't cause you to take a second look. You want to know what makes everything tick and will be doing all you can to find the answers. Personal attachments offer new diversion and exciting trips.

28 SATURDAY
Moon Age Day 12   Moon Sign Libra

There is great restlessness and mental energy to cope with this weekend but this shouldn't be a problem because it's a state of mind you are used to dealing with. Try to find something different to do – perhaps some sort of spectator sport or activity that captivates you and demands a lot of your attention. You thrive on change today.

29 SUNDAY
Moon Age Day 13   Moon Sign Libra

It's time to re-evaluate some of your objectives because what you really wanted from life only a short time ago might have changed significantly now. You are wise enough to know that everything bright and shiny isn't gold and you won't be easily fooled today by people who seem to have the answer to everyone's financial problems.

30 MONDAY
Moon Age Day 14   Moon Sign Scorpio

This would be a good time for a break from obligations. If the weight of responsibility is pressing in on you, do something completely different, take a step back and think about what you can do to relieve some of the stress. If you view situations objectively you will begin to see them in a very different and less complicated way.

♉ May 2018

Your Month at a Glance

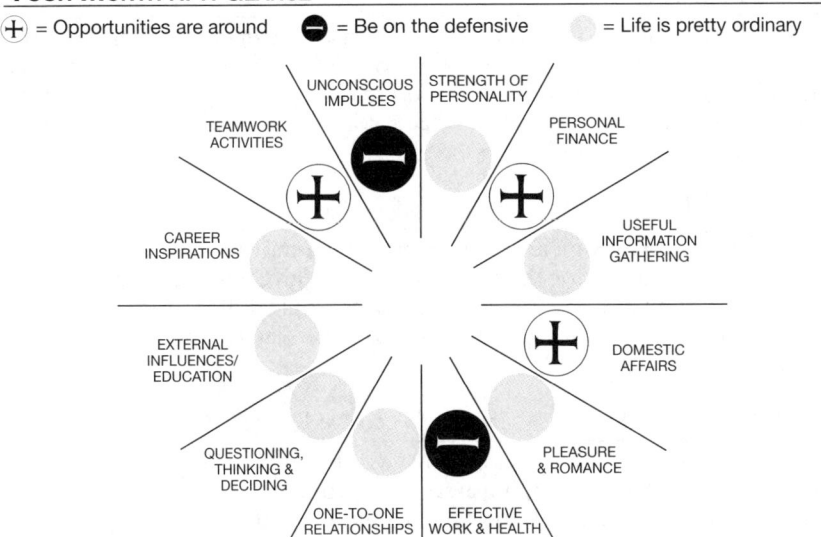

(+) = Opportunities are around   (−) = Be on the defensive   ○ = Life is pretty ordinary

- UNCONSCIOUS IMPULSES: −
- STRENGTH OF PERSONALITY: ○
- TEAMWORK ACTIVITIES: +
- PERSONAL FINANCE: +
- CAREER INSPIRATIONS: ○
- USEFUL INFORMATION GATHERING: ○
- EXTERNAL INFLUENCES/EDUCATION: ○
- DOMESTIC AFFAIRS: +
- QUESTIONING, THINKING & DECIDING: ○
- PLEASURE & ROMANCE: ○
- ONE-TO-ONE RELATIONSHIPS: ○
- EFFECTIVE WORK & HEALTH: −

May Highs and Lows

Here I show you how the rhythms of the Moon will affect you this month. Like the tide, your energies and abilities will rise and fall with its pattern. When it is above the centre line, go for it, when it is below, you should be resting.

HIGH 5TH–6TH

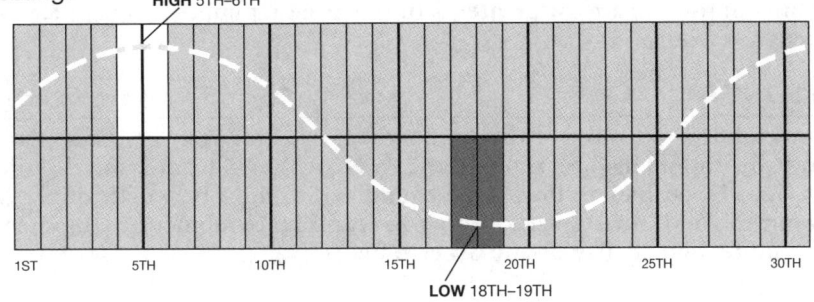

LOW 18TH–19TH

71

Your Daily Guide to May 2018

1 TUESDAY
Moon Age Day 15   Moon Sign Scorpio

You can probably afford to take life in your stride to a much greater extent around the start of May. The stressful feelings may dissipate and you could be more inclined to join in with whatever is taking place around you. There is help at hand with important decisions leading you to feel quite mellow and cheerful.

2 WEDNESDAY
Moon Age Day 16   Moon Sign Sagittarius

Insight comes to you now through instinctive feelings and you have the ability to shape your life in the way you want it to be. You know what looks and feels right and you will also be good at offering sound advice to others. Whether or not they will want to heed you remains to be seen but your involvement should be welcome.

3 THURSDAY
Moon Age Day 17   Moon Sign Sagittarius

Keep thinking and moving in equal quantity. By tomorrow you will be quieter and more reserved but for the moment you can give a good impression, no matter what company you might be in and people will be very pleased to have you around. This would also be an excellent day to push your luck in a romantic sense.

4 FRIDAY
Moon Age Day 18   Moon Sign Sagittarius

You focus on change and regeneration, which is a recurring theme in your solar chart around now. Stripping away and getting rid of unwanted situations and thought patterns needs to be part of your life, and should help you to get what you want in business situations. You appear to be in great demand now.

5 SATURDAY
Moon Age Day 19   Moon Sign Capricorn

Your desire to acquire the finer things of life is enhanced and for that you can thank the lunar high. Go for gold in all your efforts today and tomorrow and don't allow yourself to be held back by convention. The more unique you are the greater is the chance that important people will recognise you.

6 SUNDAY
Moon Age Day 20   Moon Sign Capricorn

You can now get most of the support you need for your personal plans and you should also be right in the thick of things from a social point of view. Good luck follows you around, so it might be worth thinking about the odd, small speculation. Your confidence moment-by-moment should be higher than at any other time.

Your Daily Guide to May 2018

7 MONDAY
Moon Age Day 21   Moon Sign Aquarius

Expanding and broadening your horizons should have great appeal but whatever you undertake today it is important that it has depth and meaning for you. When it comes to successes out there in the material world you won't be at all interested in hollow victories and will only want to put yourself out to achieve quite concrete results.

8 TUESDAY
Moon Age Day 22   Moon Sign Aquarius

Though you may have to overcome an initial sense of difficulty when it comes to financial and business matters, your progress today should be steady and tangible. Some ingenious ideas may help you jump over some of the stepping stones you usually have to take on the way to success.

9 WEDNESDAY
Moon Age Day 23   Moon Sign Aquarius

There are positive changes in store and some of these are likely to relate to the outdoor life. The year is moving on and the one thing you should avoid is being tied to anything that restricts you or keeps you between the same four walls. Make a bid for freedom and take anyone with you who is also restless.

10 THURSDAY
Moon Age Day 24   Moon Sign Pisces

Any sacrifices you make now are likely to be more than repaid in terms of the way others treat you in the weeks ahead. All the same, you have an increased tendency to give without any thought of repayment and you can get significant enjoyment from realising that you have helped in some small way. Your confidence is now growing.

11 FRIDAY
Moon Age Day 25   Moon Sign Pisces

You thrive on doing several tasks at the same time and you will be enjoying the cut and thrust of a busy life. Where others are concerned nothing is too much trouble for you and you undertake most tasks with a smile. People will be pleased to have you around and may ask you to volunteer.

12 SATURDAY
Moon Age Day 26   Moon Sign Aries

Now you might have to put up with what will surely be only minor aggravations but even these can be turned to your advantage if you keep smiling and remain as patient as you can be. You will enjoy a joke at the moment, even if you are on the receiving end – though it's certain that you are in the mood to give as good as you get.

13 SUNDAY *Moon Age Day 27   Moon Sign Aries*

Your practical vision should now be extremely good. You can see exactly what needs to be done and in most cases you have a really good idea about how to proceed. If there are others around who doubt your abilities they are about to get a shock. In the main you won't wait for plaudits but will simply move towards your objectives.

14 MONDAY *Moon Age Day 28   Moon Sign Taurus*

There may be some upgrading going on at work at this time and you are likely to be one of the individuals who win out as a result. If you are out of work, focus your energies and spread your search further because success is now likely. In everyday life try a little lateral thinking for maximum gain.

15 TUESDAY *Moon Age Day 0   Moon Sign Taurus*

While this is a good time to enjoy a greater degree of personal freedom, you could be somewhat fettered by the responsibility you feel towards others. There are some duties you can't get away from but, like everyone else, you do deserve a break. Problems at the moment only make you think harder to reach positive solutions.

16 WEDNESDAY *Moon Age Day 1   Moon Sign Gemini*

Some phases of your life are about to end suddenly and irreversibly but this is not a process that will come much of a surprise. This is part of a long-lasting trend that is going to find you a very different person in some ways before the summer is over. Most of the alterations are for your own good and will be welcomed.

17 THURSDAY *Moon Age Day 2   Moon Sign Gemini*

Feelings that you have kept locked away, deep inside, are now likely to rise to the surface and some of these will take you by surprise. You should have the confidence to speak out about the way you are feeling, sometimes with surprising consequences. Money matters should be settled and secure.

18 FRIDAY *Moon Age Day 3   Moon Sign Cancer*

There is now a tendency for you to do things the hard way. This is a legacy of the lunar low, though it isn't too potent this time around and is certainly not likely to have a bearing on your presently cheerful nature. Your attitude is far more easy-going than usual and some of your decisions might even shock you.

Your Daily Guide to May 2018

19 SATURDAY
Moon Age Day 4   Moon Sign Cancer

Some of your ambitions are likely to be frustrated but such is the state of play in your solar chart that you will just smile and carry on. You won't easily be depressed by outside events and there is likely to be a great deal of family support around you at present. By tomorrow the lunar low disappears and the general trends will be good.

20 SUNDAY
Moon Age Day 5   Moon Sign Leo

During this time you have a great emotional strength that extends itself around the shoulders of people who are far more vulnerable and troubled than you are. They will find great strength coming from your direction and will show their gratitude in tangible ways. Try to patch up an argument from quite some time ago.

21 MONDAY
Moon Age Day 6   Moon Sign Leo

In group activities where co-operation is required, you now show yourself at your very best. People will want to have you around and will take great joy from your presence. Get out of the house and do whatever you can to see new places and have fresh experiences. This aspect should remain important for you throughout much of the rest of May.

22 TUESDAY
Moon Age Day 7   Moon Sign Leo

Expect a fairly dynamic increase in potential but once again be somewhat careful about the decisions you make. From a financial point of view you will probably be saving rather than spending during this part of the week. That's because you know instinctively there are gains to be made if you just wait for a day or two.

23 WEDNESDAY
Moon Age Day 8   Moon Sign Virgo

Consider spending at least a little of the money you have been carefully saving for a while. The attitude of those around you is inclined to movement and activity, and you will be only too happy to join in. Don't be in the least surprised if you are singled out for some very special treatment in your social life.

24 THURSDAY
Moon Age Day 9   Moon Sign Virgo

It's time to spread your wings and also a period when you can make room for a few personal indulgences. What is the point of working and planning so hard if you never gain as a result of it? Treat yourself in some way and also involve your partner in the treat. Sharing with others is part of what makes today special.

25 FRIDAY
Moon Age Day 10   Moon Sign Libra

Socially speaking today could bring a breath of fresh air. You should be feeling that the summer has really arrived and no matter what the weather might be doing, will be lifted by the sights and sounds of the season. This would be a good day for constructive negotiations with people who have much influence.

26 SATURDAY
Moon Age Day 11   Moon Sign Libra

Don't take yourself too seriously today and you will get on better when you can smile at your own peculiarities. Let's face it, you are a unique sort of person and although you can sometimes be a stickler for habit, you are well liked and well understood by others. Enjoy a joke with friends or time at home.

27 SUNDAY
Moon Age Day 12   Moon Sign Scorpio

Feeling the need to break free from restrictions, you are at your brightest and best during most of this particular Sunday. There are gains to be made from involving yourself in social events that are planned at the last minute, though you may also be doing something that has been organised for months. This could be a busy day.

28 MONDAY
Moon Age Day 13   Moon Sign Scorpio

Today you are likely to hear something that will really cause you to sit up and take notice. It might not be much, but it is a signal for you to act, probably in terms of your financial or business life. At home you should be feeling fairly settled but don't be surprised if younger relatives give you a little cause for concern.

29 TUESDAY
Moon Age Day 14   Moon Sign Sagittarius

Someone close to you could have some information that may broaden your horizons. Listen to what is being said in your presence, because some of it is clearly intended for you. Not everyone has the courage to approach you in a direct sense. This is because Capricorn can be very self-possessed and not always immediately receptive.

30 WEDNESDAY
Moon Age Day 15   Moon Sign Sagittarius

Trends suggest that some good news could come to you from a significant distance. Not everyone will be totally honest with you at the moment, though if this is the case they are probably holding back to avoid upsetting you. Demand to know what is really going on because you work better when you do.

31 THURSDAY

Moon Age Day 16   Moon Sign Sagittarius

Don't plan anything too strenuous for today. You may be preoccupied with getting your social and personal lives running in exactly the way you want it to be. There is a just a slight inclination for you to burn the candle at both ends, which is fine for a while but tends to be wearing if you keep it up too long.

June 2018

Your Month at a Glance

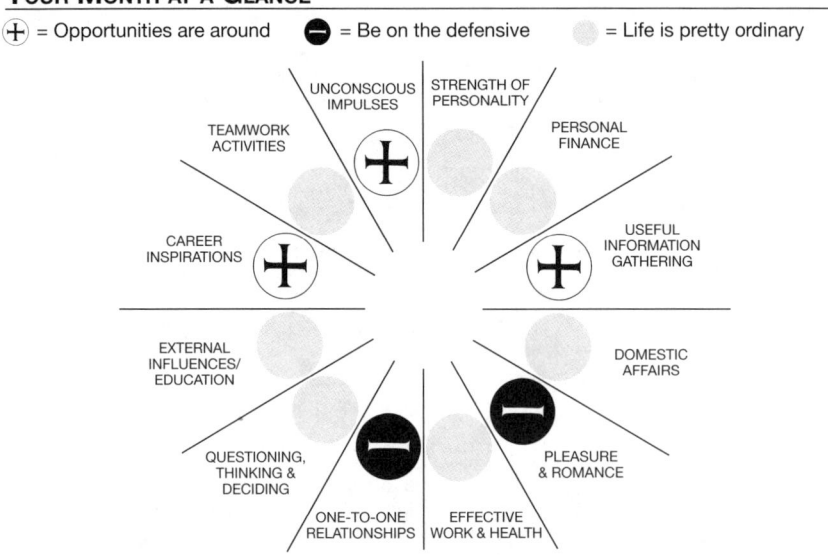

(+) = Opportunities are around   (−) = Be on the defensive   ○ = Life is pretty ordinary

- UNCONSCIOUS IMPULSES (+)
- STRENGTH OF PERSONALITY ○
- TEAMWORK ACTIVITIES ○
- PERSONAL FINANCE ○
- CAREER INSPIRATIONS (+)
- USEFUL INFORMATION GATHERING (+)
- EXTERNAL INFLUENCES/EDUCATION ○
- DOMESTIC AFFAIRS ○
- QUESTIONING, THINKING & DECIDING ○
- PLEASURE & ROMANCE (−)
- ONE-TO-ONE RELATIONSHIPS (−)
- EFFECTIVE WORK & HEALTH ○

June Highs and Lows

Here I show you how the rhythms of the Moon will affect you this month. Like the tide, your energies and abilities will rise and fall with its pattern. When it is above the centre line, go for it, when it is below, you should be resting.

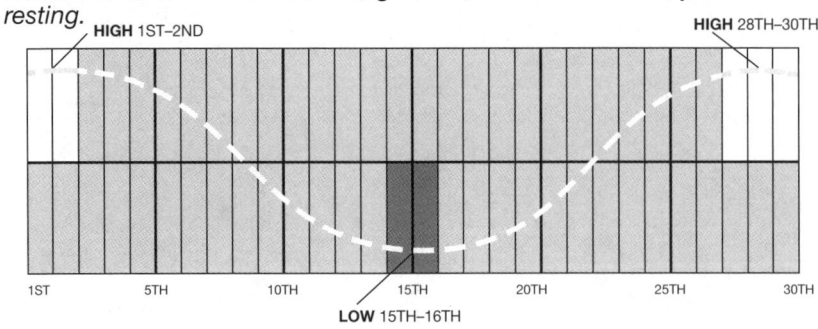

HIGH 1ST–2ND

HIGH 28TH–30TH

LOW 15TH–16TH

Your Daily Guide to June 2018

1 FRIDAY
Moon Age Day 17   Moon Sign Capricorn

You can now persuade someone much higher up the tree than you are to be of significant help to you. It appears that you have enough charm to achieve whatever you want – even when those around you will have to put themselves out wholesale on your account. The lunar high should also make you much luckier in terms of cash.

2 SATURDAY
Moon Age Day 18   Moon Sign Capricorn

Getting your own way remains easy, though there is no sign that you are bullying others into following your lead. On the contrary you will be so popular that people will queue up to do all they can for you. This is the gift of the lunar high this month and it is only sensible to use it to your advantage at every possible opportunity.

3 SUNDAY
Moon Age Day 19   Moon Sign Aquarius

This would be an ideal time to get extra work done. You should have masses of energy and no lack of incentive at the moment. Everything you do is clear and practical – just as it should be for a Capricorn. Not everyone around you is equally blessed at present so offer assistance if you can.

4 MONDAY
Moon Age Day 20   Moon Sign Aquarius

Expect to feel rather restless and it is likely that mundane tasks will be something you seek to avoid. Don't turn work versus play into any sort of problem because you now have the best capacity for mixing business with pleasure that you have experienced for some time. People will be keen to learn your opinion in most situations.

5 TUESDAY
Moon Age Day 21   Moon Sign Aquarius

Some people might consider your present style to be quite impulsive – which has to be different for usually conservative Capricorn. You are more likely to take chances and you will be keen to get your message across in a way that nobody can misunderstand. It looks as though the world will have to recognise what you are capable of achieving.

6 WEDNESDAY
Moon Age Day 22   Moon Sign Pisces

Meeting new people is favourable under present planetary trends and you will constantly be coming up with new ideas and alternative strategies for getting things done. The appreciation you have of your friends increases as they do so much to please you. Keep in touch with those who are far away.

Your Daily Guide to June 2018

7 THURSDAY
Moon Age Day 23   Moon Sign Pisces

The assurance you need from those you love might not be quite as forthcoming as you would wish but part of the trouble could be that you are not sticking around anywhere long enough to listen to what is being said. Present trends indicate that you will now be constantly on the move.

8 FRIDAY
Moon Age Day 24   Moon Sign Aries

Remove yourself from situations of potential conflict and instead of arguing spend time sorting things out on your own. This might not be easy because it is clear that you are now at your best when you are co-operating with others. The only problem now lies in the fact that you may not agree with your allies.

9 SATURDAY
Moon Age Day 25   Moon Sign Aries

Signposts to success now appear in terms of career matters. It may be that you can't do anything practical, but you can plan and make preparations, which is equally important. The responses you offer to family members will be much appreciated as you supply actual help along with verbal advice.

10 SUNDAY
Moon Age Day 26   Moon Sign Aries

There are likely to be many comings and goings today, so much so that it will be difficult to keep track of everything that is happening around you. If you stop to analyse the situation you will see that it is you who is sitting at the centre of the maelstrom and most other people are simply reacting to your demands.

11 MONDAY
Moon Age Day 27   Moon Sign Taurus

Now you can more easily advance your life by being what you naturally are. Your ability to concentrate fully, allied to a spark of inspiration that runs through your entire nature at this time will be of great use, especially in professional situations. Avoid getting frustrated with family members by talking things through rationally.

12 TUESDAY
Moon Age Day 28   Moon Sign Taurus

You now have a definite urge to become involved with things, especially in community-based projects. You feel much more like being part of a group and will be happy to put yourself out for others. You may not be the dominant factor in some situations today but you will always be there or thereabouts when the plaudits are handed out.

13 WEDNESDAY
Moon Age Day 0   Moon Sign Gemini

Group encounters are likely to work out well for you, just as long as these involve relationships of a casual rather than an intimate nature. Be flexible when it comes to getting on with colleagues and the middle of this week may bring you to a better understanding of something that remains to be done.

14 THURSDAY
Moon Age Day 1   Moon Sign Gemini

Indiscretion is not something from which you are inclined to suffer but you could be slightly less diplomatic at present than would normally be the case. The problem is that you are now more likely to speak your mind without thinking too much about the consequences, which could lead to issues and even arguments you don't really need.

15 FRIDAY
Moon Age Day 2   Moon Sign Cancer

Negative circumstances might seem to have a bearing on your life, especially in a practical sense, but once again you should think about how much you are contributing to the situation. It should be possible to sit back and watch the river of life flow by – without getting involved. The problem is that you are so committed and active at present.

16 SATURDAY
Moon Age Day 3   Moon Sign Cancer

With the lunar low comes a feeling that everyone is getting ahead much better than you are, though this is really just an illusion and has no basis in reality. Slow down and calm down because the restrictions of the lunar low can stir up trouble and angst far more than is necessary.

17 SUNDAY
Moon Age Day 4   Moon Sign Leo

You might spend some time today reliving past memories and you should be quite happy to take a break from some of the more strenuous aspects of life, if only for a day or so. People should be quite kind today and they seem to be considering your needs. This is a day for feeling generally secure.

18 MONDAY
Moon Age Day 5   Moon Sign Leo

Most of your goals are on target but there are one or two situations that require a steadier approach and more time. As a rule Capricorn is the most careful of zodiac signs but you tend to be out on a limb for now. The problem is that you don't like being told what to do, even on those occasions when you probably should be listening.

19 TUESDAY
Moon Age Day 6   Moon Sign Virgo

Today you have a great fondness for personal freedom, which is just an extension of something you have been going through for the last week or so. In your opinion the time is right to break away from the mundane and to launch yourself into something new and exciting. Any opportunity to travel should now be grasped firmly.

20 WEDNESDAY
Moon Age Day 7   Moon Sign Virgo

You seem to be very dutiful at the moment, even if underneath you long to escape from responsibility and do something that pleases only you. Part of your mind is committed to what is expected of you, but what a passion is burning away beneath the surface. Reconciling these two opposing forces might be quite hard.

21 THURSDAY
Moon Age Day 8   Moon Sign Libra

Prepare for a phase that is stimulating and exciting, with fewer possible frustrations and a greater ability to do whatever pleases you. Of course you won't be able to make all the changes your restless mind would wish, but even if you can get half way towards them you should be satisfied. Your home life should be steady and secure at present.

22 FRIDAY
Moon Age Day 9   Moon Sign Libra

Right now those higher up the tree than you are likely to be listening carefully to your ideas and will probably run with your plans. This means having to be on the ball and having all the details sorted out as quickly and efficiently as possible. That is not at all difficult for Capricorn and your intellect is as sharp as a scalpel today.

23 SATURDAY
Moon Age Day 10   Moon Sign Scorpio

The focus now is on co-operative ventures and although you can go it alone if you wish, the results will not be half as positive as they would be if you threw in your lot with others. In most situations, people will be happy to turn to you for the decision-making but you need the cohesive skills that others can provide.

24 SUNDAY
Moon Age Day 11   Moon Sign Scorpio

Now you can further your cultural and travel plans and you will find that you are fascinated by other places and different ways of living life. A range of different things can fire off your natural curiosity but it's a certainty that you are looking at aspects of the world in a new light and with great interest.

25 MONDAY
Moon Age Day 12   Moon Sign Scorpio

Career opportunities may undergo regular and quite significant changes and these will require you to keep up and to watch carefully all that is happening around you. This week is one during which you are very good at making the best of anything that is on offer and your razor-sharp mind is honed to perfection under almost all circumstances.

26 TUESDAY
Moon Age Day 13   Moon Sign Sagittarius

Expect to make a new friendship soon. It may come about as a result of your social activities, but it is highly likely that you will be joining forces with like-minded individuals in order to achieve something you see as being very important. Anything that stretches your mind will be welcomed with open arms.

27 WEDNESDAY
Moon Age Day 14   Moon Sign Sagittarius

You could feel a need to escape from the mundane responsibilities of your life but there isn't too much chance of doing so today. Stuck in the middle of the week you could feel slightly vulnerable and less inclined than usual to join in with things. Settle for a quiet evening at home and enjoy it.

28 THURSDAY
Moon Age Day 15   Moon Sign Capricorn

A realisation of personal plans is the main gift of the lunar high this time. Your general level of good luck is likely to be increased and any deals that you undertake at the moment seemed destined for success. You might be slightly impatient, especially if those close to you don't come up to expectations in their abilities.

29 FRIDAY
Moon Age Day 16   Moon Sign Capricorn

You can expect to be making personal headway and in many aspects of life you will be quite happy to go it alone if you can't get others to keep up with your frantic pace. Some colleagues or friends could consider you reckless at the moment but you know what you are doing and won't necessarily need their approval.

30 SATURDAY
Moon Age Day 17   Moon Sign Capricorn

Check out all your facts carefully but don't be too analytical of friendships or the characters of others. Don't get confused between issues but try to understand how people are likely to react to a given situation. This ability, which is almost psychic, is more in evidence at the moment than usual for you.

♑ July 2018

Your Month at a Glance

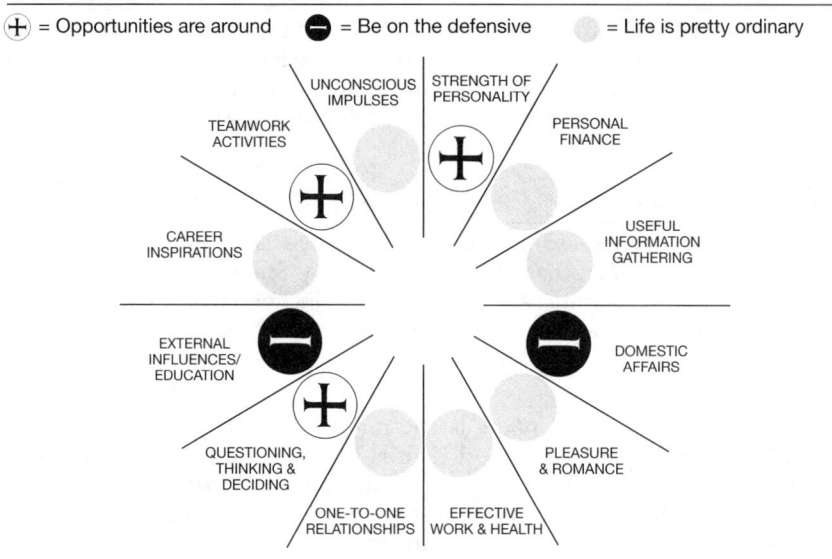

⊕ = Opportunities are around   ⊖ = Be on the defensive   ○ = Life is pretty ordinary

- UNCONSCIOUS IMPULSES
- STRENGTH OF PERSONALITY ⊕
- TEAMWORK ACTIVITIES ⊕
- PERSONAL FINANCE
- CAREER INSPIRATIONS
- USEFUL INFORMATION GATHERING
- EXTERNAL INFLUENCES/EDUCATION ⊖
- DOMESTIC AFFAIRS ⊖
- QUESTIONING, THINKING & DECIDING ⊕
- PLEASURE & ROMANCE
- ONE-TO-ONE RELATIONSHIPS
- EFFECTIVE WORK & HEALTH

July Highs and Lows

Here I show you how the rhythms of the Moon will affect you this month. Like the tide, your energies and abilities will rise and fall with its pattern. When it is above the centre line, go for it, when it is below, you should be resting.

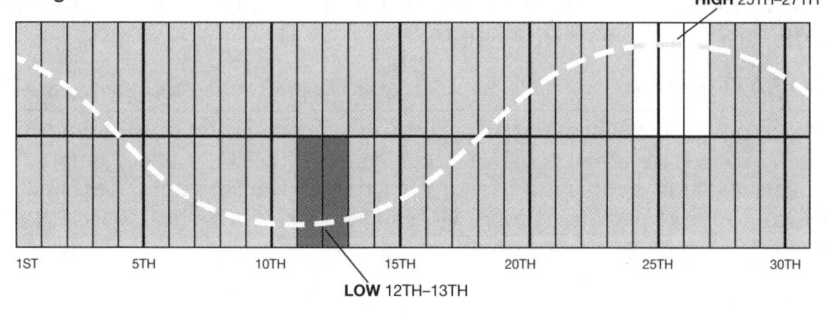

HIGH 25TH–27TH
LOW 12TH–13TH

84

Your Daily Guide to July 2018

1 SUNDAY
Moon Age Day 18   Moon Sign Aquarius

This is a day when you should concentrate on reliable, long-term relationships and find the time to make a special fuss of your partner. You are likely to be in a fairly nostalgic frame of mind and at the same time you hand out kindness to most of those who are important to you.

2 MONDAY
Moon Age Day 19   Moon Sign Aquarius

Community involvement becomes more important and you will also continue your present drive to support the underdog. This will happen both at work and later in your social life. Your consideration is likely to extend to those people you don't know at all and your charitable intentions could take on a whole new meaning in your life.

3 TUESDAY
Moon Age Day 20   Moon Sign Pisces

You are quite energetic under present trends and won't be at all put out by undertaking several different projects at the same time. If there is one thing that Capricorn possesses it is long-term stamina. You may not be the fastest individual in the world but once you get going all the king's horses and men could not stop you.

4 WEDNESDAY
Moon Age Day 21   Moon Sign Pisces

Now you may enjoy an even higher profile in social situations and your influence is very strong. You can play the role of team leader very well and because you are so confident at present people are more likely than ever to turn to you for guidance. There are also possible gains to be made in terms of your finances.

5 THURSDAY
Moon Age Day 22   Moon Sign Pisces

There is a chance you will be too competitive for your own good just at present, which can turn out to be a bind if you accidentally tread on the toes of other people. Co-operation is definitely better than competition and it will not be difficult to find ways to involve others in your endeavours. You can even delegate at present.

6 FRIDAY
Moon Age Day 23   Moon Sign Aries

Your interaction with groups, societies and associates is likely to be quite enjoyable today and may form an important part of your social life. Friendship brings much improved communication and you have something to say that will be of interest to almost anyone. Don't forget appointments that were made a long time ago.

7 SATURDAY
Moon Age Day 24   Moon Sign Aries

Your ideas should find positive support today, even from people you haven't always thought of as being natural allies. Your sense of justice is reflected back at you as colleagues and friends offer you the benefit of the doubt, even when they suspect you could be wrong. It's time to shine for Capricorn.

8 SUNDAY
Moon Age Day 25   Moon Sign Taurus

Today is likely to find you as the centre of attention, which might sometimes worry you but is unlikely to bother you much at present. The great advantage about the planetary line-up at the moment is that it allows you to be popular and active but also inspires you to think deeply and to plan ahead.

9 MONDAY
Moon Age Day 26   Moon Sign Taurus

You are professionally suited to tasks that leave you free to do things in the way you think is best. Make your own decisions and though you are also quite happy to give others the lead, expect to be unhappy if they make demands of you. This becomes ever more obvious in situations that are likely to arise right now.

10 TUESDAY
Moon Age Day 27   Moon Sign Gemini

Perhaps you want to introduce a little more variety into your everyday life and you certainly have the planetary positions around you to make this possible. Optimistic and idealistic at present, you won't have any time for people who have underhand or dubious motives. You will be defensive of your friends.

11 WEDNESDAY
Moon Age Day 28   Moon Sign Gemini

Your imagination can be your greatest asset now because, generally speaking, if you think it you can probably do it too. There are very few limitations being placed upon you and your mind is now less fettered than would sometimes be the case. The only slight fly in the ointment might be somewhat garbled communications.

12 THURSDAY
Moon Age Day 29   Moon Sign Cancer

With the lunar low comes a definite slowing in the pace of your life but this will somehow seem to be quite natural and timely. As a result this could be the least potent lunar low of the year so far. The only real piece of advice worth following right now is to hesitate before implementing far-reaching changes.

13 FRIDAY
Moon Age Day 0   Moon Sign Cancer

Don't be surprised if there are slight hardships or minor disappointments taking place at home. These are phantoms that will most likely reverse themselves within a day or two. In any case, you are apt to worry about situations that are not worth the effort. This is a very temporary return of the negative Capricorn you can occasionally be.

14 SATURDAY
Moon Age Day 1   Moon Sign Leo

You can get great pleasure from meeting new people and from being constantly on the move. This would be a fine time for travel and you should be enjoying the fact that summer has well and truly arrived. What won't appeal to you at the moment is being stuck in the same place and undertaking routine tasks all day.

15 SUNDAY
Moon Age Day 2   Moon Sign Leo

You should be entertaining company today, which is why others are so happy to have you around. Your general level of confidence remains high and the Sun in its present position is part of the reason. This would be another good time to travel so this is the perfect time for Capricorns to take a holiday.

16 MONDAY
Moon Age Day 3   Moon Sign Virgo

You now excel in testing situations and this could turn out to be one of the most potent working weeks for some time. Where decisiveness and action are required you show just how capable you are and you should be right on the ball when it comes to decision-making. These are qualities you display in all spheres of your life now.

17 TUESDAY
Moon Age Day 4   Moon Sign Virgo

Someone at work may anger you today but it would be just as well to keep your temper. You will be better able to deal with situations if you view them dispassionately, rather than flying off the handle. At home things are likely to be better and you may be reaching a new understanding with your partner.

18 WEDNESDAY
Moon Age Day 5   Moon Sign Libra

You should be feeling quite optimistic and outgoing. Even if you are not getting quite as much done as you would wish you probably won't worry too much. In some ways you could be slightly torn between being productive and at the same time achieving the level of social interaction that is presently possible.

19 THURSDAY
Moon Age Day 6   Moon Sign Libra

Although this remains a generally good and high-spirited sort of day, be aware that not everyone will think that you are quite as important as you do. You now have a slight tendency to be quite elevated in your own estimation, something that happens to Capricorn now and again. Try a little extra humility.

20 FRIDAY
Moon Age Day 7   Moon Sign Libra

Intense emotions at the moment are likely to strengthen your love life and give you even more reason than usual to tell those closest to you how you really feel about them. A good heart-to-heart talk with just about anyone seems to be the way forward today and you will be so sincere in what you are saying everyone will believe you.

21 SATURDAY
Moon Age Day 8   Moon Sign Scorpio

Professionally, you should be going more or less where you want to be, but of course this is the weekend and what matters most today are the social and personal aspects of your life. Positive results are likely, especially when you turn your full attention in a specific direction. Love should be especially heart-warming now.

22 SUNDAY
Moon Age Day 9   Moon Sign Scorpio

Possessing tremendous energy at the moment, you probably can't do enough to satisfy your own needs of yourself. In some ways you could be pushing too hard. Don't forget that this is a Sunday, which is supposed to be a day of rest. Leave some time aside to spend with your partner and to entertain younger family members.

23 MONDAY
Moon Age Day 10   Moon Sign Sagittarius

At this time you should be able to fulfil some of your most important desires, though there are also some that will have to wait. You could be rather too impatient for your own good in certain respects, so a degree of patience would also help. What you aren't keen to do right now is spend all day merely assisting someone else.

24 TUESDAY
Moon Age Day 11   Moon Sign Sagittarius

Certain matters still require more patience and perseverance than you are willing to give them. Everything will seem to take you longer than you would wish and you will really have to put in the hours if you want to be certain of getting exactly what you want. Later in the day you should put the worries away and have a good time.

Your Daily Guide to July 2018

25 WEDNESDAY
Moon Age Day 12   Moon Sign Capricorn

You can now outwit any competition and you arrive at your conclusions quickly and with little effort. You really should try your luck today, though of course in a limited way because you are, after all, a Capricorn. You don't have to believe in everything you do today. All that is necessary is to become involved.

26 THURSDAY
Moon Age Day 13   Moon Sign Capricorn

Stick to your guns when you feel that something is important because you exude such power at the moment people around you are not likely to argue. This means you will generally get your own way and can do so without making enemies. A little psychology goes a long way, as you are about to discover to your advantage.

27 FRIDAY
Moon Age Day 14   Moon Sign Capricorn

There's a great wanderlust within you starting today and you won't be satisfied to merely stay in the same place and do the same old things. On the contrary, you are in the mood for change and excitement – a legacy of the present planetary line-up. Enlist the support of someone close to you and do something quite outrageous.

28 SATURDAY
Moon Age Day 15   Moon Sign Aquarius

Now is the time to bring something to a suitable conclusion. This is especially true in terms of your career. Trying to concentrate totally on what you should be doing won't be all that easy because there are so many potential diversions surrounding you at this time. Put your best foot forward and get onside with people who are in the know.

29 SUNDAY
Moon Age Day 16   Moon Sign Aquarius

You can now easily overcome slightly negative emotional trends and you do so by sharing your innermost feelings with your lover. Capricorns who are looking for a new love are likely to be more successful in their endeavours now, mainly because you are using a more ingenious method in order to get what you are searching for.

30 MONDAY
Moon Age Day 17   Moon Sign Pisces

Your thought processes should be now be clear and concise. You are quite calculating in your judgements yet at the same time you will be good company and anxious to keep making the sort of good impression on others that can count. Today should be varied in what it offers, with plenty of stimulation and interest.

31 TUESDAY *Moon Age Day 18   Moon Sign Pisces*

You will now be more willing to give and also more willing to listen to what other people are saying. This isn't universally the case for Capricorn because once you decide how things ought to be, you automatically assume that everyone around you will agree. New issues on the social front will lift your spirits later.

August 2018

Your Month at a Glance

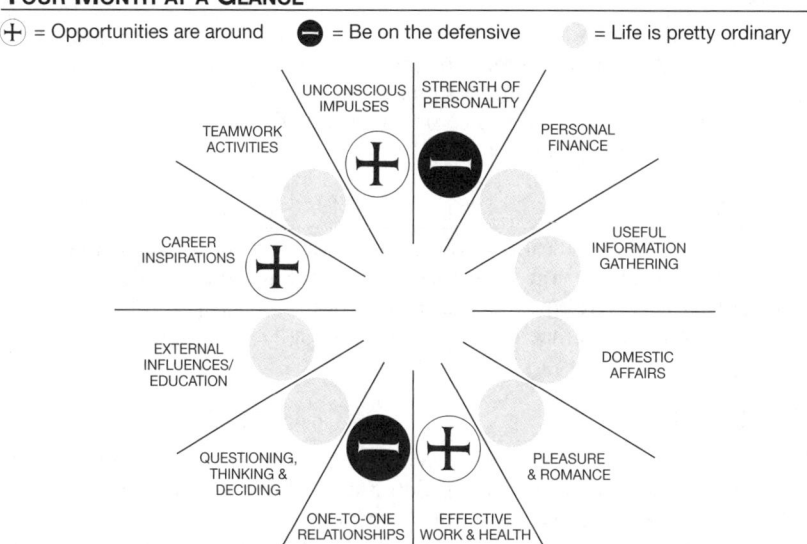

⊕ = Opportunities are around   ⊖ = Be on the defensive   ○ = Life is pretty ordinary

- UNCONSCIOUS IMPULSES ⊕
- STRENGTH OF PERSONALITY ⊖
- TEAMWORK ACTIVITIES
- PERSONAL FINANCE
- CAREER INSPIRATIONS ⊕
- USEFUL INFORMATION GATHERING
- EXTERNAL INFLUENCES/ EDUCATION
- DOMESTIC AFFAIRS
- QUESTIONING, THINKING & DECIDING ⊖
- PLEASURE & ROMANCE ⊕
- ONE-TO-ONE RELATIONSHIPS
- EFFECTIVE WORK & HEALTH

August Highs and Lows

Here I show you how the rhythms of the Moon will affect you this month. Like the tide, your energies and abilities will rise and fall with its pattern. When it is above the centre line, go for it, when it is below, you should be resting.

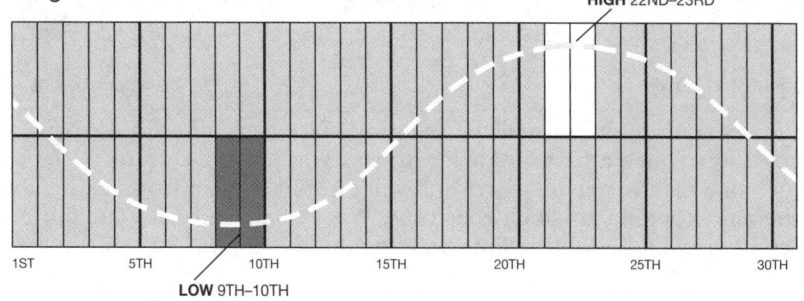

HIGH 22ND–23RD

LOW 9TH–10TH

1ST   5TH   10TH   15TH   20TH   25TH   30TH

91

Your Daily Guide to August 2018

1 WEDNESDAY ☿   *Moon Age Day 19   Moon Sign Pisces*

Your sway over others may not be quite as strong for the next few days as it seems to have been recently. Actually this may be something of an illusion because your influence remains potent but generally hidden. It isn't the things you are doing directly that count but the successes that don't show on the surface.

2 THURSDAY ☿   *Moon Age Day 20   Moon Sign Aries*

You have keen powers of observation and you assess most situations in a moment. Avoid allowing yourself to dwell on matters from the past and. in particular, don't let your mind wander to what you consider to have been unfair treatment you received once upon a time. The present and the future are all that should really matter.

3 FRIDAY ☿   *Moon Age Day 21   Moon Sign Aries*

There can be some irritation coming your way, especially associated with your finances. Perhaps you have made a mistake in your calculations or it could be that there are unexpected bills coming in. It is possible that some of these could relate to machinery or electrical gadgets but you will just have to pay up and look happy.

4 SATURDAY ☿   *Moon Age Day 22   Moon Sign Taurus*

All the benefits of teamwork activities are now there for the taking. Participating in group endeavours is definitely to be recommended, not least of all because you are so sociable and giving at the moment. Be specific with the advice you are offering to younger family members and make sure they listen.

5 SUNDAY ☿   *Moon Age Day 23   Moon Sign Taurus*

It would be quite easy now to lose yourself in some flight of fancy or another. Normally clear ideas can seem somehow fuzzy for the moment and you are not as decisive as you would wish. None of this is likely to bother your partner because it appears you have a lot of romance in your soul at the moment.

6 MONDAY ☿   *Moon Age Day 24   Moon Sign Gemini*

It looks as though you will be meeting some very interesting types of people on your path through life today. You are unlikely to be in too much of a rush to get anywhere and will most likely gain from taking your time and stopping to smell the roses. With excursions on your mind at present you could even be doing so literally.

Your Daily Guide to August 2018

7 TUESDAY ☿ *Moon Age Day 25   Moon Sign Gemini*

There are some aspects of life that you can now afford to take for granted – though probably not for long. You find yourself at a crossroads in some respects and many of the challenges that lie ahead of you are ones you will choose for yourself. Don't be surprised if you are singled out for special attention at work.

8 WEDNESDAY ☿ *Moon Age Day 26   Moon Sign Gemini*

Financial opportunities could now allow you to organise your life better and will add to the sense of security you are always anxious to feel. There is nothing worse for Capricorn than to worry about money and with such concerns out of the way for a while you can concentrate on gaining from all that this lovely month has to offer.

9 THURSDAY ☿ *Moon Age Day 27   Moon Sign Cancer*

Obstacles can be thrown in your path at a moment's notice and the lunar low becomes all the more apparent this time simply because you have been cruising along so successfully. It is unlikely that anything would challenge you for any length of time because other planets are so powerful they blow away doubt or anxiety.

10 FRIDAY ☿ *Moon Age Day 28   Moon Sign Cancer*

Various circumstances continue to work in your favour but there could be a sort of discontent within you today that is difficult to identify. Trying to stay one step ahead of any game won't be easy and you might have to rely on intuition as much as you will on your customary practical common sense. Look up old friends today.

11 SATURDAY ☿ *Moon Age Day 0   Moon Sign Leo*

You may be able to excel in whatever sort of work you are doing at the moment. You seem to have the right qualifications to get ahead and people will trust you to instinctively. They don't do this on a whim. Capricorn is one of the most reliable and trustworthy signs of the zodiac and especially so at present.

12 SUNDAY ☿ *Moon Age Day 1   Moon Sign Leo*

You tend to enjoy the good life and all that is fine and luxurious now. This is the side of Capricorn that marks it out as a true Earth sign and you will do your best at the moment to look as good as possible. This is especially the case when you appear in social situations. The sort of entries you make would be worthy of royalty.

13 MONDAY ☿ *Moon Age Day 2 Moon Sign Virgo*

You should now focus on the world of education, travel and culture. Present trends stimulate your mind and your ability to communicate your ideas and emotions to others is much increased. This carefree attitude is slightly at odds with what many people expect from you but nobody is likely to complain about the diversion.

14 TUESDAY ☿ *Moon Age Day 3 Moon Sign Virgo*

This is a time during which personal plans are more positively highlighted than would usually be the case. You are willing to discuss your ideas with just about anyone and will look far and wide to find an audience if one is not immediately to hand. Versatility is the best key to success under present trends and you have it in legions.

15 WEDNESDAY ☿ *Moon Age Day 4 Moon Sign Libra*

Your impact on others remains positive and it is clearly the right time to show the social world who you are and how confident you can be. At work you are likely to be happy-go-lucky and probably quite inspirational in your general approach. You should have no doubt about anything you undertake today.

16 THURSDAY ☿ *Moon Age Day 5 Moon Sign Libra*

There are now unexpected and quite original ways to make money. Business opportunities are likely to involve friends and some Capricorns will be choosing this time to make wholesale changes to their professional lives. Perhaps you are being headhunted, or else you have just come up with the most wonderful idea imaginable.

17 FRIDAY ☿ *Moon Age Day 6 Moon Sign Scorpio*

Differences of opinion are possible today but it really just depends on the way you approach people and also on how you listen to what they are trying to tell you. There is usually a compromise possible but if you are up against formidable negotiators you will have to work hard to reach it. It might be best to wait until later.

18 SATURDAY ☿ *Moon Age Day 7 Moon Sign Scorpio*

You should find that you are well able to cope with more than one project at once today. The ability to think in several different directions is latent to all Capricorns, but is showing up especially well under present astrological trends. As a result you might decide it would be best to avoid limiting yourself.

19 SUNDAY
Moon Age Day 8   Moon Sign Sagittarius

Though this is still a time when you can get ahead, there are certain limitations. Maybe you feel you are not getting through to others in the way you would wish and want to make a better impression. It appears that you might be facing anxieties that are unrealistic and a little common sense goes a long way.

20 MONDAY
Moon Age Day 9   Moon Sign Sagittarius

Others appear to be getting ahead quicker than you are, though this observation might have no validity at all once you really get yourself into gear. Be as objective as possible and don't allow minor aggravations to get in your way. Good times are on the way personally and financially, so look out for them.

21 TUESDAY
Moon Age Day 10   Moon Sign Sagittarius

You probably cannot avoid being quieter for the moment, which is a response to a twelfth house Moon. Because you are more contemplative you will have time to plan ahead, which could turn out to be advantageous. Some of your social contacts may be drying up and if you want to get them back a little action will be necessary soon.

22 WEDNESDAY
Moon Age Day 11   Moon Sign Capricorn

It could be said that this is a period for throwing caution to the wind and for putting all your effort in specific directions. The lunar high gives you greater energy and a determination to get where you most want to be. This is an especially good time for travel, even if you are embarking on journeys planned at a moment's notice.

23 THURSDAY
Moon Age Day 12   Moon Sign Capricorn

There is a positive focus on where you are going and how you intend to get there. Recent trends have been quite helpful and this can be a landmark year for Capricorn. Today offers renewed incentives, better prospects on the personal front and a degree of popularity amongst your friends that can really put you centre stage.

24 FRIDAY
Moon Age Day 13   Moon Sign Aquarius

Look out for a boost related to all influences concerning home and family. This is not to suggest that you are moving backwards in your work, merely that any spare time you do have is apt to be dedicated to those you love the most. If you have been on some sort of health kick, keep up the effort because you will feel better for it soon.

25 SATURDAY
Moon Age Day 14   Moon Sign Aquarius

There are likely to be some minor setbacks today and there probably isn't a great deal you can do about it except to be patient. Allow others to take some of the strain, whilst you sit back and watch for once. Best of all you could let a little luxury into your life after a very busy time. The idea today is to watch and wait.

26 SUNDAY
Moon Age Day 15   Moon Sign Aquarius

Trends quickly move on and now you can expect a period of great positive gains and forward-looking optimism. This is a time when you take life by force in many respects. Focus at least some of your attention on creating new ways to have fun. Avoid getting involved in disputes that are not going to get you anywhere and stay cool.

27 MONDAY
Moon Age Day 16   Moon Sign Pisces

It looks as though love will be firmly on the horizon for some Capricorns. If you are looking for a relationship, this is one of the periods of the year during which it would be sensible to keep your eyes open. Even everyday friendship can offer a good deal more than seems to have been the case of late so look at them closely.

28 TUESDAY
Moon Age Day 17   Moon Sign Pisces

Love and romantic developments should be quite important on this August Tuesday. Because things might be slightly quieter in some ways, you have time to look at intimate associations in a new light. If there is one issue that is firmly on your mind today, deal with it as soon as you can – then relax.

29 WEDNESDAY
Moon Age Day 18   Moon Sign Aries

Continue to strive for personal happiness and to take as many others in that direction as you can. This is no time to allow your mind to work overtime, unless of course that means that you are turning dreams into reality. All sorts of contacts with others are likely to be enhanced by present trends and new attachments should be sound.

30 THURSDAY
Moon Age Day 19   Moon Sign Aries

It may not be easy to keep up with the demands of your nearest and dearest, particularly on an emotional level. Capricorn is usually patient, but this quality seems to be taking a holiday for a day or two. All in all, it might be better to spend time on your own rather than upsetting others unintentionally.

31 FRIDAY
Moon Age Day 20   Moon Sign Aries

Don't miss any opportunity at this time, especially when it comes to making yourself more comfortable in some way. In public situations allow yourself to shine and don't worry about a few people not assisting the process. All in all this could turn out to be a sparkling end to the working week.

September 2018

Your Month at a Glance

⊕ = Opportunities are around   ⊖ = Be on the defensive   ● = Life is pretty ordinary

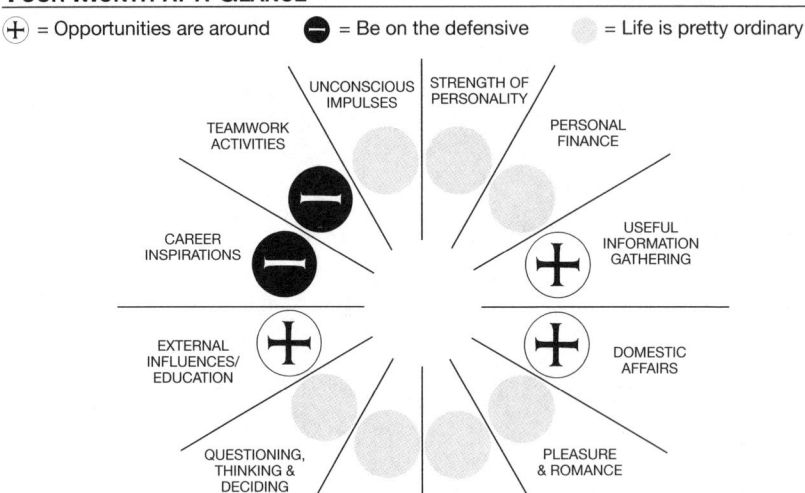

- UNCONSCIOUS IMPULSES
- STRENGTH OF PERSONALITY
- TEAMWORK ACTIVITIES ⊖
- PERSONAL FINANCE
- CAREER INSPIRATIONS ⊖
- USEFUL INFORMATION GATHERING ⊕
- EXTERNAL INFLUENCES/ EDUCATION ⊕
- DOMESTIC AFFAIRS ⊕
- QUESTIONING, THINKING & DECIDING
- PLEASURE & ROMANCE
- ONE-TO-ONE RELATIONSHIPS
- EFFECTIVE WORK & HEALTH

September Highs and Lows

Here I show you how the rhythms of the Moon will affect you this month. Like the tide, your energies and abilities will rise and fall with its pattern. When it is above the centre line, go for it, when it is below, you should be resting.

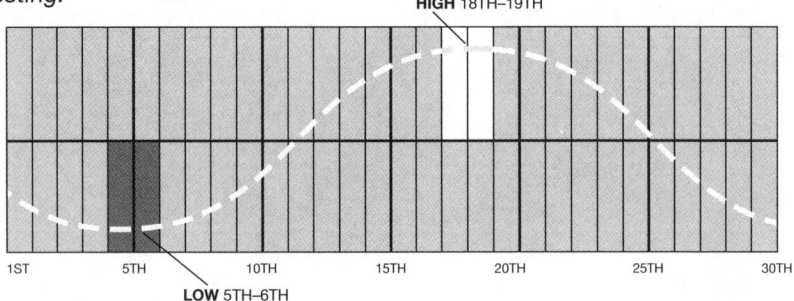

HIGH 18TH–19TH

LOW 5TH–6TH

Your Daily Guide to September 2018

1 SATURDAY
Moon Age Day 21   Moon Sign Taurus

You may discover some fairly unexpected solutions to some of life's little problems today and it is clear that your foresight is good. It may even appear that you are psychic because you seem to see so clearly ahead of yourself. Others recognise this too and might be calling on your skills to assist them in their own lives.

2 SUNDAY
Moon Age Day 22   Moon Sign Taurus

Your potential for making money is likely to be reaching a peak and you should not turn down any opportunity that comes your way to add to your bank account. Capricorns who are not working at present will probably have better luck with job-seeking today and some of your problems may now vaporise.

3 MONDAY
Moon Age Day 23   Moon Sign Gemini

This is a day when you can afford to take as many chances as possible. You will enjoy a very high profile amongst your friends and associates and people will actively do all they can to have you around. Whilst the Sun remains in its present position you will be in the market for change and for getting to grips with old problems too.

4 TUESDAY
Moon Age Day 24   Moon Sign Gemini

If you lack anything at the moment it is likely to be mental flexibility. Be as open as possible to new ideas and once you have understood them, incorporate them into your life. There is no point at all in hanging on to situations from the past or in keeping up any sort of pretence just for the sake of those around you.

5 WEDNESDAY
Moon Age Day 25   Moon Sign Cancer

You will now be far more reluctant to show how innovative you can be and would be more likely to stick stubbornly to what you know and trust. Although you are unlikely to suddenly turn into a hermit and isolate yourself altogether from the world it is likely that you will be happiest with your own company for a day or two.

6 THURSDAY
Moon Age Day 26   Moon Sign Cancer

Although you have to be on your guard to counter setbacks things generally are not half as difficult as they might tend to look right now. Your points of reference are not exactly ideal and you are more pessimistic than you have been across the last few weeks. By tomorrow you should be back to a more positive frame of mind.

Your Daily Guide to September 2018

7 FRIDAY
Moon Age Day 27   Moon Sign Leo

This would be an ideal time to surround yourself with friends and to use the skills they have to further your own objectives, as well as theirs. Partnerships of almost any sort are likely to work well and there could be excitement around every corner. Get out of doors as much as possible and enjoy the world at this time of year.

8 SATURDAY
Moon Age Day 28   Moon Sign Leo

Practical developments continue to provide benefits and current plans should move you closer and closer towards ultimate success. The greatest emphasis right now should be on having fun but there is no reason why you should not enjoy what is going on around you, while at the same time finding ways to gain from it.

9 SUNDAY
Moon Age Day 0   Moon Sign Virgo

Your curiosity is likely to be provoked today and this could lead to some eyebrow-raising news. While others seem oblivious to the ultimate conclusions of their actions you see clearly ahead and will be turning over all stones in your desire to be informed. This tendency will certainly give you the edge when it comes to business.

10 MONDAY
Moon Age Day 1   Moon Sign Virgo

Other people may notice the breathless pace of your life at this time more than you do. You are so busy dashing from pillar to post and back again that you won't stop long enough to recognise the way you look when viewed by your colleagues and friends. Never mind, it is better to get things done while you are in the right mood.

11 TUESDAY
Moon Age Day 2   Moon Sign Libra

You have a natural charm at the moment that is so infectious people will want to be with you as much as possible. When you are put into positions of authority you tend to lead by example and not by throwing your weight around. You represent Capricorn at its most charming and could make some friends now.

12 WEDNESDAY
Moon Age Day 3   Moon Sign Libra

Opportunities for progress lie in finance and business as September continues. Your potential for gaining more in a financial sense is good and there are rewards on the way for Capricorns who are willing to take a few small, calculated risks. You will be at your very best now when you are the company of intellectual equals.

Your Daily Guide to September 2018

13 THURSDAY
Moon Age Day 4   Moon Sign Scorpio

Keep your eyes and ears open and jump at any chance to make today your own, right from its very start. There is likely to be new information coming in from friends and associates that you can use to your own advantage. Don't get too tied up with family problems, particularly since most of them may be insignificant.

14 FRIDAY
Moon Age Day 5   Moon Sign Scorpio

If you lack anything at the moment it is likely to be mental flexibility. Be as open as possible to new ideas and once you have understood them, incorporate them into your life. There is no point at all in hanging on to situations from the past or in keeping up any sort of pretence just for the sake of those around you.

15 SATURDAY
Moon Age Day 6   Moon Sign Scorpio

A period of harmonious communication comes along and it could not have done so on a better day of the week. You will have both the time and the incentive to spend some hours with your loved ones, especially your partner. Outside the home, new alliances can be formed and you begin to understand someone better.

16 SUNDAY
Moon Age Day 7   Moon Sign Sagittarius

This is a time of independence and a period when you won't take kindly to others telling you what you should be doing. One particular job you have embarked upon might seem to be taking a very long time but the effort you put in will certainly be worthwhile and you show great resilience at the moment.

17 MONDAY
Moon Age Day 8   Moon Sign Sagittarius

Amongst colleagues you could find one or two people who don't approve of your methods or the way you want to do something. Although you are quite patient at the moment and will probably do your best to explain yourself, in the end you will most likely feel that you have little choice but to carry on in your own sweet way.

18 TUESDAY
Moon Age Day 9   Moon Sign Capricorn

This would be a great time for seeking promotion or for doing something at home that makes you feel far less restricted and more in control of your own destiny. You could be feeling very popular in a social sense because it certainly seems as if everyone wants to have you around. Make use of this by asking for a few little favours.

19 WEDNESDAY *Moon Age Day 10   Moon Sign Capricorn*

Moves made now, either socially or professionally, are likely to turn to your advantage. You have plenty of energy and an even greater determination to get ahead in life. New dreams and schemes replace those that have fallen by the wayside and there is almost nothing to prevent you from achieving your objectives at present.

20 THURSDAY *Moon Age Day 11   Moon Sign Aquarius*

The best aspects of life at this stage of the week are social ones. Although you can get everything done that you need to in a business and a practical sense, in the main you will be happiest when you are able to enjoy yourself in good company. This is another good time for travel and a September holiday would suit you no end.

21 FRIDAY *Moon Age Day 12   Moon Sign Aquarius*

Your natural intuition allows you to notice everything that is going on around you and all without deviating one step from the path you want to take. It doesn't matter what people actually say because you see clear through to the truth of most situations. It would take someone really good to fool you in any way.

22 SATURDAY *Moon Age Day 13   Moon Sign Aquarius*

You should be optimistic, cheerful and very confident at this time. Don't wait in the wings to be asked to do anything because now is the time to take what you need, whilst charming everyone around you on the way. Even if you put a foot wrong you have what it takes to make others believe you were right all along.

23 SUNDAY *Moon Age Day 14   Moon Sign Pisces*

Build on your recent efforts today. Don't start anything new but make sure you are dealing with existing issues in the best way possible. The attitude of a friend might surprise you and you will have to talk things through carefully so as not to upset someone who is very sensitive. Material gains look likely at this time.

24 MONDAY *Moon Age Day 15   Moon Sign Pisces*

Beware because too much false optimism could get in your way, at least at the start of today. You need to be quite critical, both of yourself and of situations you don't entirely understand. Don't take anything to pieces today unless you are absolutely sure how you should go about putting it together again.

25 TUESDAY
Moon Age Day 16   Moon Sign Aries

Most aspects of life should suit you for the moment and you will be working in conjunction with others to achieve common objectives. There could still be one or two doubters around but in the main you are well accepted and your views will be taken into account. This is especially true in the case of superiors.

26 WEDNESDAY
Moon Age Day 17   Moon Sign Aries

You now have an uncanny ability to attract most of what you need and you do so without any real fuss or bother. The bossy side of Capricorn is now taking a holiday and you are both compliant and easy-going. There might be a quieter spell to come so it would be sensible to put the finishing touches to certain jobs today if you can.

27 THURSDAY
Moon Age Day 18   Moon Sign Aries

Friends and loved ones might not approve of the way you deal with a specific issue today, though you are a great thinker and can usually win out in any discussion. On the other hand, perhaps they are right and this might be a good time to look at things afresh. Even Capricorn can't be right all the time.

28 FRIDAY
Moon Age Day 19   Moon Sign Taurus

Today you should be in a good position to be in possession of knowledge that can help you to move forward with your finances. You are certainly paying attention and won't have much difficulty establishing the facts you need in order to live your life successfully. Friends may be demanding but you probably won't mind.

29 SATURDAY
Moon Age Day 20   Moon Sign Taurus

This continues to be a beneficial period with regard to money and property. You should now realise that getting what you want from life involves far less effort and trouble than is sometimes the case and you might even wonder at the way you are dealing with obstacles that got in your way just a few days ago.

30 SUNDAY
Moon Age Day 21   Moon Sign Gemini

On the last day of September you could again be focusing on monetary considerations and it's true that you have some strong support in your solar chart at the moment when it comes to making more cash. You have good ideas and might ally yourself to people who are experts in fields you don't understand. Co-operation is the key.

October 2018

Your Month at a Glance

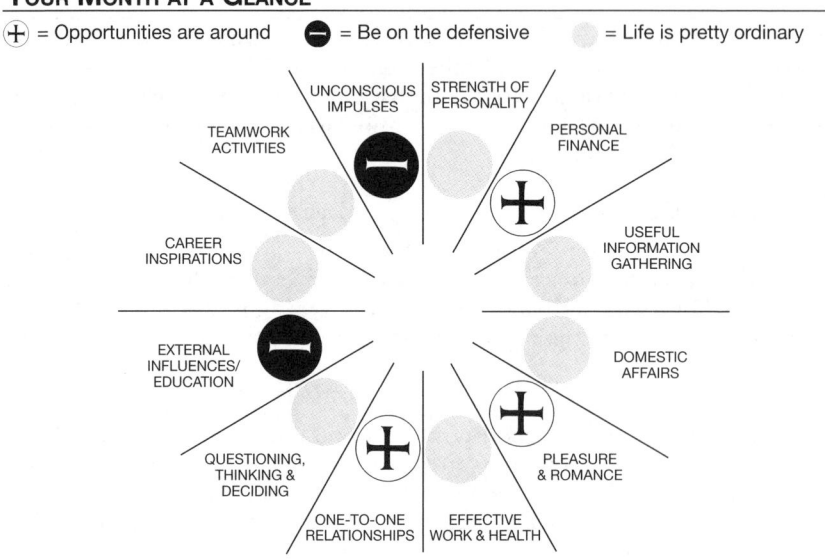

(+) = Opportunities are around   (−) = Be on the defensive   ○ = Life is pretty ordinary

- UNCONSCIOUS IMPULSES — (−)
- STRENGTH OF PERSONALITY — ○
- TEAMWORK ACTIVITIES — ○
- PERSONAL FINANCE — (+)
- CAREER INSPIRATIONS — ○
- USEFUL INFORMATION GATHERING — ○
- EXTERNAL INFLUENCES/EDUCATION — (−)
- DOMESTIC AFFAIRS — ○
- QUESTIONING, THINKING & DECIDING — ○
- PLEASURE & ROMANCE — (+)
- ONE-TO-ONE RELATIONSHIPS — (+)
- EFFECTIVE WORK & HEALTH — ○

October Highs and Lows

Here I show you how the rhythms of the Moon will affect you this month. Like the tide, your energies and abilities will rise and fall with its pattern. When it is above the centre line, go for it, when it is below, you should be resting.

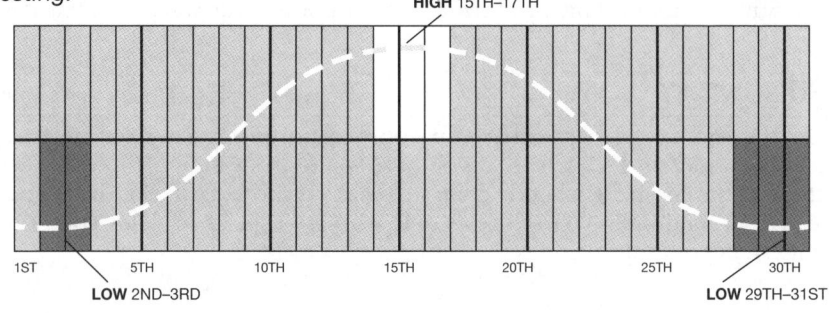

HIGH 15TH–17TH

LOW 2ND–3RD

LOW 29TH–31ST

104

Your Daily Guide to October 2018

1 MONDAY
Moon Age Day 22   Moon Sign Gemini

You should find it easier to get your own way this week. If there are issues that you feel need resolving, especially in the personal sphere, now is the time to tackle them head on. In a financial sense, some of the finer things in life that you have been hoping might come your way are not likely to be all that far away.

2 TUESDAY
Moon Age Day 23   Moon Sign Cancer

There could be a slightly sluggish start to today, brought about in the main by the lunar low. However, the demands you make of life are not all that great and if you keep a fairly low profile the lunar low may pass you by quietly. Seek new forms of entertainment and keep your mind occupied if you can.

3 WEDNESDAY
Moon Age Day 24   Moon Sign Cancer

Curb your ambitions as much as possible and leave some of the major decisions that are waiting in the wings for just a little longer. Dig out information from the past when it seems obvious that your former actions can have a bearing on the present but don't let yourself become too nostalgic because some sorrow could be the result.

4 THURSDAY
Moon Age Day 25   Moon Sign Leo

Today should be good in terms of your resources because you are likely to get on top of your spending and could coming up with some ingenious plans to hang on to money in the medium and long-term. You have the ability to look far ahead of yourself at this time and will be almost prophetic in your thoughts and actions.

5 FRIDAY
Moon Age Day 26   Moon Sign Leo

It appears that you will now be more anxious than ever to learn and to put what you have learned to good use in very practical ways. You remain extremely receptive to other people's ideas and will be able to move comfortably towards major objectives. You won't try to do everything all at once because you have patience par excellence.

6 SATURDAY
Moon Age Day 27   Moon Sign Virgo

Standing up for what you believe is right should not be too difficult under present trends and you can be quite courageous when the will takes you. This is more likely to be the case when you are defending those you love and since this is also a great time for romance it is likely to be the sphere of personal attachments that you prosper.

Your Daily Guide to October 2018

7 SUNDAY
Moon Age Day 28   Moon Sign Virgo

A positive belief in your own worth is vitally important if you want to wring as much as you can out of practical and business matters at this time. If you stand around, jumping from foot to foot, rivals may slip in and steal the prize. You need to be decisive but also to appear as cool as possible. It's a tall order but achievable.

8 MONDAY
Moon Age Day 29   Moon Sign Virgo

There is a continued emphasis on work and productivity and this must surely mean that things are happening around you. You have a big attitude to life at the moment and you may even be quite dramatic in the way you do things. People love to see the passionate side of your nature on display.

9 TUESDAY
Moon Age Day 0   Moon Sign Libra

Although rules and regulations might tend to get on your nerves you will realise, as you always do, that these are necessary to your happiness. It is likely that you will be quite original in your thinking, especially at work, and you show your very practical side on most occasions. Save time later in the day for important words of love.

10 WEDNESDAY
Moon Age Day 1   Moon Sign Libra

Patience is the keyword for Capricorn now. Everything you want can come your way eventually but much of it will be nothing more than potential under present trends. If you rush your fences now you might prevent an eventual success, whereas watching and waiting until the right moment will ensure you get what you are seeking.

11 THURSDAY
Moon Age Day 2   Moon Sign Scorpio

Dream up new and important projects for the future and lay the foundations of later actions one by one. Today can offer significant social diversion and you may have a great desire to be outdoors. From a physical point of view you could become involved in sporting activities, especially team sports.

12 FRIDAY
Moon Age Day 3   Moon Sign Scorpio

Though progress is now likely to be swift there is so much happening at the same time you may need a little assistance in order to make the best of it all. That means relying on other people, something you are occasionally loath to do. This stems from a feeling that if you want something doing right you must do it yourself – but this isn't the case.

13 SATURDAY
Moon Age Day 4   Moon Sign Sagittarius

You would certainly rather speak than listen today, which is why you have so much to say in almost any situation. Part of this is a nervous response on your part and it is also the case that you want to feel you are in command of everything. If there are things you don't understand today you could become quite frustrated.

14 SUNDAY
Moon Age Day 5   Moon Sign Sagittarius

You can protect your sense of your own identity in an original way today and may inspire others through your ability to be unique and to constantly turn in directions they don't expect. This should assure you of attention but will also lead to significant successes in your life. Little things turn your way under present trends and make for an interesting time.

15 MONDAY
Moon Age Day 6   Moon Sign Capricorn

Opportunities for expansion come along as the Moon races into your own sign of Capricorn. This is the time of the month to commit yourself to new projects and to show just how confident you are capable of being. The more you extend yourself the greater is the degree of confidence and help that is going to come from other people.

16 TUESDAY
Moon Age Day 7   Moon Sign Capricorn

This is one of the best days of the month for making important decisions and you won't want to be left behind when there is excitement on offer. Not only will you be very confident but it is likely that you will feel on top from in a physical sense too. Good fortune can play an important part in the way things pan out, especially at work.

17 WEDNESDAY
Moon Age Day 8   Moon Sign Capricorn

This ought to be a very favourable time indeed for getting on with those around you in a general sense. If not all the conversations you are having seem to possess the depth you would wish, who cares? There is nothing wrong with a little superficiality, just as long as you get what you need in the end. Stay cheerful and optimistic today.

18 THURSDAY
Moon Age Day 9   Moon Sign Aquarius

You may feel today that the pressure is somehow on in terms of relationships. This could show itself in any one of a number of different ways. Perhaps family members are more demanding, or your partner is worrying about specific issues. Whatever turns up, deal with it steadily and don't panic about anything.

19 FRIDAY　　　　　　　　　　　Moon Age Day 10　Moon Sign Aquarius

Your ability to attract just the right sort of people at this time is noteworthy. Keep yourself active, happy and geared towards situations that are reasonable. Friends should be of greater assistance now and they offer you the chance to follow a course of action that has seemed out of the question recently.

20 SATURDAY　　　　　　　　　　Moon Age Day 11　Moon Sign Pisces

You might have to give in to other people today more than you would wish but to be willing to do this now means greater progress later. Personal attachments should be looking especially good and you will have the time today to follow up on a couple of issues that have been put on the back burner since before last weekend.

21 SUNDAY　　　　　　　　　　　Moon Age Day 12　Moon Sign Pisces

Discussions with others ought to prove fairly interesting today. If you do not work on a Sunday there is scope for social trends to win out. Maybe you are planning a family trip or a party? Whatever you turn your mind to now should be successful later. Your cheerfulness impresses everyone

22 MONDAY　　　　　　　　　　　Moon Age Day 13　Moon Sign Pisces

You may now be entering a slightly up and down sort of period but it is one that offers all sorts of new incentives and plenty of diversity. If there are issues that need dealing with today you can be sure that you will sort these out quite quickly, especially if you are willing to fall back on the experience of relatives.

23 TUESDAY　　　　　　　　　　　Moon Age Day 14　Moon Sign Aries

Beware of getting hold of the wrong end of the stick when it comes to a personal matter. Although you think you are listening to others, you are probably not hearing exactly what they are trying to tell you. There are some deceptions around today, mostly coming from colleagues or people you don't know well.

24 WEDNESDAY　　　　　　　　　Moon Age Day 15　Moon Sign Aries

All you require today in order to make life go with a swing is a little extra incentive and some positive thinking. If things are not sorted out the way you would wish them to be, this is the time to put in that extra effort to help yourself. There are offers of support from colleagues and friends but you might not want to accept it.

25 THURSDAY
Moon Age Day 16 Moon Sign Taurus

Iron out problems with colleagues and make sure you do so before you move forward into a potential minefield of issues. Today is probably not the best time for concerted action because you tend to be in a very thoughtful frame of mind. Wait until tomorrow before you really begin to apply the pressure to any situation.

26 FRIDAY
Moon Age Day 17 Moon Sign Taurus

You are motivated by all sorts of new ideas and incentives at the end of this working week and there isn't any doubt that you have a great deal to contribute in a general sense. Not everyone understands what you are talking about today so in amongst the successes it would be worth explaining yourself just a little more carefully

27 SATURDAY
Moon Age Day 18 Moon Sign Gemini

The daily routine will offer you a sense of stability and peace. Feeling at ease with yourself, you should be equally comfortable with everyone else around you. You enjoy their company and can make the most of the strong social trends that are surrounding you on all sides. Personal attachments should also look quite secure.

28 SUNDAY
Moon Age Day 19 Moon Sign Gemini

Any negotiations should proceed quickly and easily, mainly because you are so accommodating and also willing to stretch your own ideas to encompass those of other people. Hybrid solutions work extremely well and Capricorn is so co-operative at this time you could be forming alliances with unexpected people.

29 MONDAY
Moon Age Day 20 Moon Sign Cancer

You may feel a little unsure today and probably not on top form at the start of another week. The lunar low could hold you back a little and it could seem as though the things you want the most are still a long way off. By the middle of the week everything will look different so just exercise a little patience now.

30 TUESDAY
Moon Age Day 21 Moon Sign Cancer

Although you will want to make some necessary changes today, the time is probably not quite right yet. Look at situations today and do all the planning you want but wait for a while before you put your plans into action. This is because you will soon find new ways to cope with issues that are still puzzling you at the moment.

31 WEDNESDAY *Moon Age Day 22   Moon Sign Cancer*

Good intuition should enable you to see ahead of yourself and will prevent you from making some of the mistakes that could come along otherwise. Turn up the heat of your love and let your special one know how you are feeling and continue to show as much of a co-operative spirit as you can. This is a mixed day but a good one.

November 2018

Your Month at a Glance

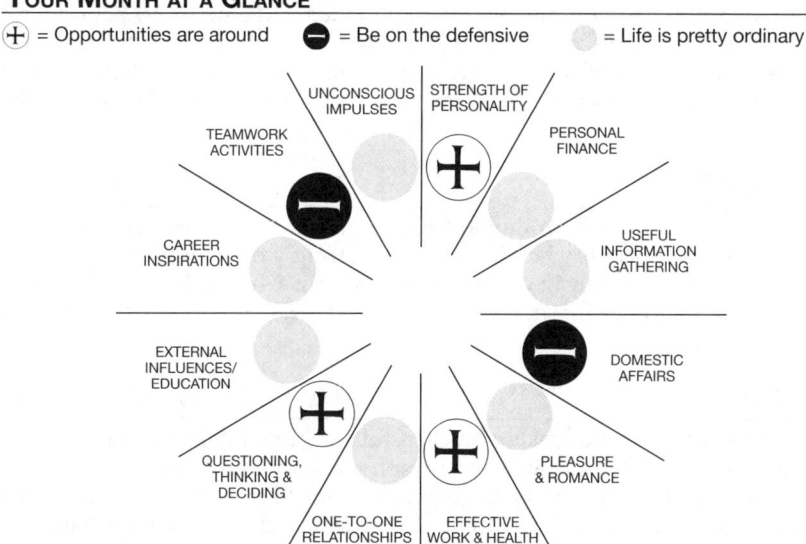

(+) = Opportunities are around   (−) = Be on the defensive   ○ = Life is pretty ordinary

- STRENGTH OF PERSONALITY: +
- PERSONAL FINANCE: ○
- USEFUL INFORMATION GATHERING: ○
- DOMESTIC AFFAIRS: −
- PLEASURE & ROMANCE: +
- EFFECTIVE WORK & HEALTH: ○
- ONE-TO-ONE RELATIONSHIPS: +
- QUESTIONING, THINKING & DECIDING: ○
- EXTERNAL INFLUENCES/EDUCATION: ○
- CAREER INSPIRATIONS: ○
- TEAMWORK ACTIVITIES: −
- UNCONSCIOUS IMPULSES: ○

November Highs and Lows

Here I show you how the rhythms of the Moon will affect you this month. Like the tide, your energies and abilities will rise and fall with its pattern. When it is above the centre line, go for it, when it is below, you should be resting.

HIGH 12TH–13TH

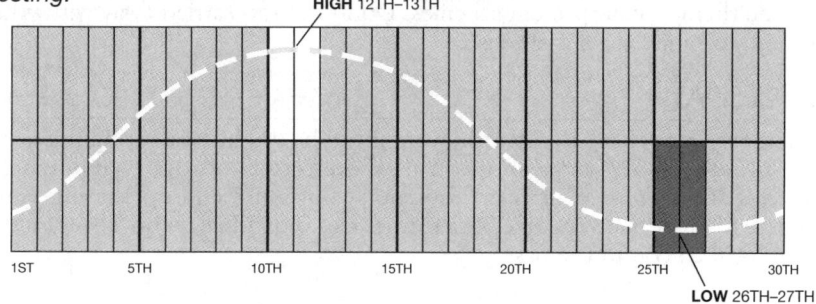

LOW 26TH–27TH

111

1 THURSDAY
Moon Age Day 23   Moon Sign Leo

You are possessed of considerable mental talents at the best of times but this really shows now. This is a time to stretch yourself and to explore new avenues. Your objectives may be self-evident but what matters around now is the newer and better ways you think up to get where you want to be.

2 FRIDAY
Moon Age Day 24   Moon Sign Leo

You have a need for communication of all kinds and a desire to get on with life to its fullest. There are several planets now contributing to the push you are about to make and with everything going your way, be willing to urge yourself forward. This might not always be easy but it certainly seems to be necessary.

3 SATURDAY
Moon Age Day 25   Moon Sign Virgo

All areas of communication should still be going well and this weekend could be especially important when it comes to getting what you want from love. Your popularity is hardly in doubt and Capricorns who are looking for a new romance should concentrate their efforts on social contacts and invitations this weekend.

4 SUNDAY
Moon Age Day 26   Moon Sign Virgo

A communicative trend makes you cheerful and approachable. Not everyone you get on well with today will be a person you have taken to in the past. You might have to re-write the book regarding your likes and dislikes of certain individuals and you could even discover a former adversary who is happy to join forces with you.

5 MONDAY
Moon Age Day 27   Moon Sign Libra

Someone at home could be making life more vibrant for you around now. There is excitement in the air and it is coming from a number of different directions. Stay loyal to the people who have been kind to you in the past and include them in your present schemes. Don't get too carried away with your own importance in a social sense.

6 TUESDAY
Moon Age Day 28   Moon Sign Libra

What loved ones have to offer today ought to be doubly reassuring but keep certain plans under wraps until you are more certain of your own potential success. If you play your hand too soon you could end up sharing your gains with too many people. Stick to those individuals who have always been loyal to you in the past.

Your Daily Guide to November 2018

7 WEDNESDAY
Moon Age Day 0   Moon Sign Scorpio

Expect a harmonious time, especially in the way you are getting on with loved ones, friends and colleagues alike. You have what it takes to heal breaches, even if they are ones you did nothing to create in the first place. Capricorn is now not likely to apportion blame to anyone or hold a grudge.

8 THURSDAY
Moon Age Day 1   Moon Sign Scorpio

You should now discover that attracting the money you need is somewhat easier, partly because others have so much confidence in what you have to say. Your own private nest egg should be growing and if you check all the accounts carefully it is quite possible you will discover you are better off then you thought.

9 FRIDAY
Moon Age Day 2   Moon Sign Sagittarius

You should not allow anything to interfere with the normal flow of business. This is an excellent time to emphasise how practical you are capable of being and it looks as though a wealth of people will be offering their own resources to support you. Not everyone is presently on your side but the people who really matter should be.

10 SATURDAY
Moon Age Day 3   Moon Sign Sagittarius

You now have a much better insight into your own thinking and it could be that you begin to realise important things about yourself that haven't occurred to you before. Domestic relationships should be especially rewarding but you also need to be out there in the wider world so it is vital that you split your time successfully today

11 SUNDAY
Moon Age Day 4   Moon Sign Sagittarius

Work and money matters are positively highlighted right now and it looks as though you will find that getting what you want from life is significantly easier at this stage of November than sometimes seems to be the case. In reality you are moving small mountains without realising that they even exist!

12 MONDAY
Moon Age Day 5   Moon Sign Capricorn

This may prove to be one of your busiest periods as far as work is concerned. With plenty to think about and everything to play for you are likely to be right on form and keen to show your mettle. You won't rely on good luck because you are working so hard but don't be surprised if things turn your way more or less of their own accord.

Your Daily Guide to November 2018   ♑

13 TUESDAY *Moon Age Day 6   Moon Sign Capricorn*

Casual conversations and communications of all sorts can be turned in a moment to your advantage and you show all day long just how ingenious you are. There are new starts in the offing, not to mention situations that test you to the full. All in all, you should positively enjoy what life throws at you.

14 WEDNESDAY *Moon Age Day 7   Moon Sign Aquarius*

At home it looks as though emotional extremes might be somewhat difficult to avoid. A minor crisis could at least release pent-up emotions and you are almost certain to speak your mind at the moment, no matter what the implications might be. Get together with like-minded friends to ring the changes and reduce the intensity.

15 THURSDAY *Moon Age Day 8   Moon Sign Aquarius*

You may be bored by your own domestic routines so look for inventive ways to get the most from all that is happening around you now. It is possible that you are failing to pick up on a number of opportunities and you need to look carefully at all the new possibilities that are starting to gather around you.

16 FRIDAY *Moon Age Day 9   Moon Sign Aquarius*

The pull of the past is likely to be very strong today and you will be fairly nostalgic about certain events. This isn't an entirely bad thing because there are possible lessons to be learned for the future. In relationships you are loyal and not at all demanding, which seems to indicate a good period romantically.

17 SATURDAY ☿ *Moon Age Day 10   Moon Sign Pisces*

You can make this a time of positive change, even if you have to take care not to try and move forward in too many areas at the same time. Friends have good ideas, some of which you will want to help them explore and it looks as though some quite fascinating news could come in from the direction of someone you don't know yet.

18 SUNDAY ☿ *Moon Age Day 11   Moon Sign Pisces*

Make plans today and set out to learn new skills. Don't allow yourself to be held back by irrelevant details and look at the overall picture for once. Sunday should be good for your social life, and you have a good ability at this time to mix business with pleasure – to your definite profit.

Your Daily Guide to November 2018

19 MONDAY ☿ — *Moon Age Day 12   Moon Sign Aries*

Though you might have to overcome a slight sense of inertia at the beginning of this week you can gain ground in terms of domestic issues. If you feel you want to be more comfortable ahead of the winter, this might be a good time to make alterations at home. Some DIY should appeal to you now.

20 TUESDAY ☿ — *Moon Age Day 13   Moon Sign Aries*

The main area of pleasure and fulfilment remains with your home and family. Of course you cannot be there all the time but even when you are not, that is the direction in which your thoughts tend to run. Personal attachments seem to offer a greater sense of security than ever – which is something Capricorn always needs.

21 WEDNESDAY ☿ — *Moon Age Day 14   Moon Sign Taurus*

There could be fruitful encounters with a range of different people today, some of whom have an important message to pass to you. Gradually, you should notice that things are speeding up. There are gains to be made in terms of your money-making potential and your thought processes are likely to be keener than ever.

22 THURSDAY ☿ — *Moon Age Day 15   Moon Sign Taurus*

Financial, legal and career matters should all be going quite well. If the time has come to sign documents of any sort or to take on a new commitment, you are in the best frame of mind to deal with such issues right now. Friends should be supportive and on occasions probably rather too helpful for your liking.

23 FRIDAY ☿ — *Moon Age Day 16   Moon Sign Taurus*

Positive thinking rules today and that has to be good for Capricorn, which sometimes lacks the ultimate commitment to move ahead in a confident way. Even when you are not sure of something, nobody around you would guess at the moment. You can bluff your way through anything and gain more and more confidence as you move forward.

24 SATURDAY ☿ — *Moon Age Day 17   Moon Sign Gemini*

Relationships with family members could improve – even if you aren't especially aware that anything has been wrong with them. In one or two cases there might have been a certain distance developing in what was once a water-tight attachment and you should soon see that everything is back to normal. Look after cash today.

25 SUNDAY ☿ — Moon Age Day 18   Moon Sign Gemini

Along with a greater sense of self-determination, your energy levels pick up today. You are likely to be the main attraction in social groups and will be happy to occupy that position. Any doubts or uncertainties are left behind and you move forward in the knowledge that you really do know what you are doing.

26 MONDAY ☿ — Moon Age Day 19   Moon Sign Cancer

You may struggle to achieve your ends for a couple of days but that doesn't mean you should avoid putting in the effort or give up altogether. Even moderate progress is better than no movement at all. Later in the day, set plenty of time aside to rest while the lunar low is around.

27 TUESDAY ☿ — Moon Age Day 20   Moon Sign Cancer

Now is not the time to allow your confidence to get out of control. There are certain ideas that are presently sloshing about in your mind and this quiet spell gives you the chance to review them one by one. You may be slightly socially reluctant and will probably find your own fireside to be the most appealing place outside of work.

28 WEDNESDAY ☿ — Moon Age Day 21   Moon Sign Leo

You can now make progress on home improvement projects and find ways to make yourself feel more settled and happy in your surroundings. You have good insight when it comes to your working life and you will already have one eye on the end of the year – a time at which certain of your plans come to fruition.

29 THURSDAY ☿ — Moon Age Day 22   Moon Sign Leo

You are now entering a phase of radical alteration to both your ideas and your actions. Nothing much is likely to happen today but you are putting new ideas into place and your mind is going down paths you probably have not explored before. Every small step you take leads you to newer and more exciting places.

30 FRIDAY ☿ — Moon Age Day 23   Moon Sign Virgo

It might be said that Capricorn is now even more in tune with its own feelings than it has probably been for the last month or two. You should be fairly satisfied with the way things are going in a general sense, though you may decide that there isn't enough variety in your social life. If you make changes, take others into account.

December 2018

Your Month at a Glance

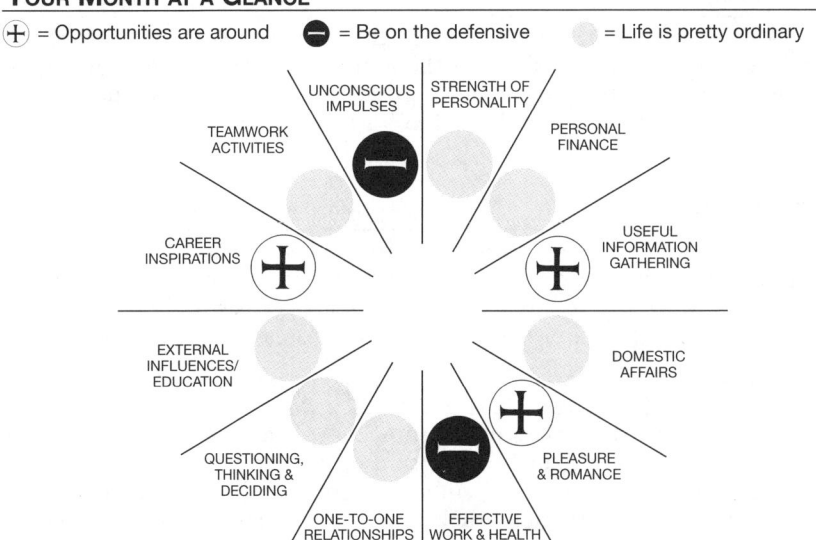

⊕ = Opportunities are around   ● = Be on the defensive   ○ = Life is pretty ordinary

- UNCONSCIOUS IMPULSES — ●
- STRENGTH OF PERSONALITY
- TEAMWORK ACTIVITIES
- PERSONAL FINANCE
- CAREER INSPIRATIONS — ⊕
- USEFUL INFORMATION GATHERING — ⊕
- EXTERNAL INFLUENCES/ EDUCATION
- DOMESTIC AFFAIRS
- QUESTIONING, THINKING & DECIDING
- PLEASURE & ROMANCE — ⊕
- ONE-TO-ONE RELATIONSHIPS
- EFFECTIVE WORK & HEALTH — ●

December Highs and Lows

Here I show you how the rhythms of the Moon will affect you this month. Like the tide, your energies and abilities will rise and fall with its pattern. When it is above the centre line, go for it, when it is below, you should be resting.

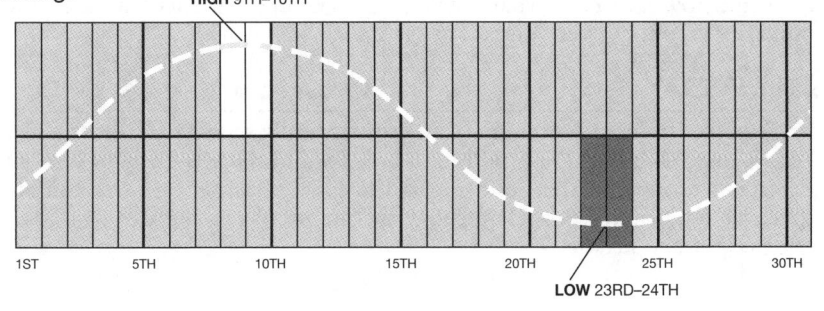

HIGH 9TH–10TH

LOW 23RD–24TH

117

Your Daily Guide to December 2018

1 SATURDAY ☿ *Moon Age Day 24   Moon Sign Virgo*

Although you want to push on in a general sense you will probably have to be more aware of your own limitations today and that could mean having to rely on the good offices of those around you to a much greater extent than you normally would. There is a slight danger that you could allow your imagination to run away with you.

2 SUNDAY ☿ *Moon Age Day 25   Moon Sign Libra*

You now need a domestic atmosphere that is both warm and secure – a response to the present position of the Sun in your chart. There should be plenty of opportunity to relax and a great desire on your part to be kind to family members and friends. It looks as though you already have that Christmas spirit ahead of time.

3 MONDAY ☿ *Moon Age Day 26   Moon Sign Libra*

The desires of others could clash somewhat with your own needs and wants today and that might lead to a dispute or two. If so you can be fairly sure of getting your own way because you are extremely persuasive right now. Work issues could seem like heavy demands but other areas will be less stressed.

4 TUESDAY ☿ *Moon Age Day 27   Moon Sign Scorpio*

What a good time this would be for showing off and for convincing others that you are equal to just about any task they want to set you. From a social point of view you love places of entertainment and should willingly join in with pre-Christmas gatherings such as carol concerts or the local school Nativity play.

5 WEDNESDAY ☿ *Moon Age Day 28   Moon Sign Scorpio*

Home is a great place for entertaining at the moment and there is little doubt that you will be happier there than anywhere else. You may not have quite the level of drive that was evident a week or two ago but you are a great host right now and have what it takes to make everyone feel at ease. Your popularity is running very high.

6 THURSDAY ☿ *Moon Age Day 29   Moon Sign Scorpio*

This can be quite an exciting time romantically. Many Capricorns will already be getting into the mood for a holiday and there is likely to be some excitement around in the build-up to the Christmas period. You can also expect recognition of your talent today and an interest in many of your ideas, even the outrageous ones.

Your Daily Guide to December 2018

7 FRIDAY
Moon Age Day 0   Moon Sign Sagittarius

You could encounter a little conflict with people in authority today. You are not in a mood to listen to what you think is nonsense and you are likely to say so, no matter who you are dealing with. Take care that you don't do or say something that could lead to you cutting off your nose to spite your face.

8 SATURDAY
Moon Age Day 1   Moon Sign Sagittarius

This is a day when you will want to relax a little and improve your surroundings. Although you might be committed to work during the day, once the responsibilities are out of the way you will be spending some time planning for the future. This is one of Capricorn's favourite pastimes so you should be quite happy.

9 SUNDAY
Moon Age Day 2   Moon Sign Capricorn

Generally speaking you should be in for a good time today and tomorrow. The lunar high finds you on top form and anxious to enjoy yourself, no matter what you happen to be doing. Put your best foot forward and do all that is necessary to make life better and easier. Finances are likely to be stronger than they have been for quite a while.

10 MONDAY
Moon Age Day 3   Moon Sign Capricorn

This is a favourable time for luck and personal growth. In quite a few ways the world should be opening up to you and the chance of you gaining ground at work especially is particularly strong. There are new gifts and blessings likely to be on the way and some of them come in such a disguised form it takes a while to recognise them.

11 TUESDAY
Moon Age Day 4   Moon Sign Aquarius

When it comes to the more personal side of your life, you could be going through something of a quiet revolution at the moment. You are looking very deeply at attachments and the way you have been responding to them. Changes may have to be made but these are all likely to be for the better in the end.

12 WEDNESDAY
Moon Age Day 5   Moon Sign Aquarius

Working within a team environment should suit you no end today. You have lots to offer and will be more co-operative than usual. There are times when Capricorn wants to be in charge and this can sometimes lead to conflict. For the moment you will be quite happy to brainstorm with almost anyone and you will relish the results.

Your Daily Guide to December 2018

13 THURSDAY
Moon Age Day 6   Moon Sign Aquarius

There is now less pressure about than could have been the case yesterday and you are more likely to drop back into an easy-going phase. The rest of the month is going to offer some very comfortable periods and times when you are focused equally on the past and the future. For today at least, the present is your best resort.

14 FRIDAY
Moon Age Day 7   Moon Sign Pisces

Opportunities that arise today are likely to take you in completely new directions. Although you have masses of energy and can get a great deal done, in the main you won't need to push yourself too hard. Lady Luck smiles on you and this makes it easy for you to achieve your objectives without too much effort.

15 SATURDAY
Moon Age Day 8   Moon Sign Pisces

Your relaxed and sociable attitude during this part of December is likely to be very infectious. You may be starting the Christmas round already and probably socialising with colleagues and friends alike. This is a good time for low-key networking and for coming up with new schemes that can be played out after Christmas.

16 SUNDAY
Moon Age Day 9   Moon Sign Pisces

Try to be as laid back as you can about domestic arrangements because everything seems to be running quite smoothly. If you are particularly nervous about something you have arranged, go over the details with a friend and then you can relax. In company you are charming, your nature is well balanced and you shine.

17 MONDAY
Moon Age Day 10   Moon Sign Aries

At work you will probably still be very busy. If you are retired or between jobs at the moment you will be equally busy at home. Plans go ahead for new social encounters and there is plenty to get done across the next few days. In some ways you might discover that you are too active for your own good. Slow down a little.

18 TUESDAY
Moon Age Day 11   Moon Sign Aries

High spirits continue to prevail and you can be the life and soul of any party – some of which you are quite happy to be organising. You have a strong impact on others and usually for their good but you can be just a little bossy when you come across situations you think are pointless or stupid. Try to be understanding today.

Your Daily Guide to December 2018

19 WEDNESDAY
Moon Age Day 12   Moon Sign Taurus

Though your ego is quite strong today, you turn this to your advantage. There is no likelihood of you taking a back seat in anything during today and if there are new games to be played, you will definitely want to win. Split the day between family members and friends but don't try to do more than is sensible.

20 THURSDAY
Moon Age Day 13   Moon Sign Taurus

It might feel as though something about today is missing. Maybe you have forgotten to get in touch with someone or it could be that a particular friend has not been around recently. A little careful thought should put matters right and since you are especially good at organising today, get your sleeves rolled up.

21 FRIDAY
Moon Age Day 14   Moon Sign Gemini

Involvements in the social and romantic arena ought to prove rewarding now. Get out and meet others and try as many new things as you can. It's time for you to generally show off because you have much that others find attractive. What's more you will happily enjoy the limelight at present, without feeling in the least conspicuous.

22 SATURDAY
Moon Age Day 15   Moon Sign Gemini

Loved ones and all social connections prove to be important right now and with Christmas up ahead you may suddenly realise how many things you haven't done. That doesn't matter. What counts today is realising how much love surrounds you and making the most of it. You will be on good form socially towards the end of the day.

23 SUNDAY
Moon Age Day 16   Moon Sign Cancer

Stand by for a slightly sluggish period now that the lunar low has arrived. Look at this as a good thing as you will get it out of the way before Christmas actually arrives. You will need to rely a lot today on the good offices of others and if there is something you simply cannot do you will need to enlist the support of a professional.

24 MONDAY
Moon Age Day 17   Moon Sign Cancer

This is not the most suitable time to tempt fate by taking on risky propositions. Keep life steady and stick to what you know best. Grandiose schemes should wait until after today, by which time you will have forgotten about them anyway. Friends should prove to be loyal and supportive, and may want to draw you into everything.

Your Daily Guide to December 2018

25 TUESDAY
Moon Age Day 18   Moon Sign Leo

This is likely to be a romantic Christmas Day for many Capricorns. Your commitment to that someone special is particularly strong but you have more than enough affection to share out amongst family members and friends. There could be gifts on the way that you certainly never expected to get.

26 WEDNESDAY
Moon Age Day 19   Moon Sign Leo

Family and domestic matters are probably more rewarding today than they have been since the start of the Christmas holidays. There may be less incentive around to be on the go and there are gains to be made from staying in one place for a while and talking to family members. Plans for future journeys could easily be laid down today.

27 THURSDAY
Moon Age Day 20   Moon Sign Virgo

You could have to do a lot of rushing around today because it is just possible you are trying to balance a busy period at work with a much-enhanced social life. Romance is also centre stage at this time and you might be reappraising your approach to someone you fancy. You have a very positive attitude generally.

28 FRIDAY
Moon Age Day 21   Moon Sign Virgo

With significant changes coming along in your attitude – especially with regard to practicalities, you are quite inspirational in your thinking and actions today. At the same time you will want to indulge your fancies somewhat and will probably choose to spend time in the company of people you find to be intelligent and inspirational.

29 SATURDAY
Moon Age Day 22   Moon Sign Libra

You have a strong desire to expand your boundaries today and may already be tiring of all the parties and especially the mince pies. You want to get yourself back into gear but that won't be entirely possible until after the end of the year. For the moment, plan and keep yourself busy with social events.

30 SUNDAY
Moon Age Day 23   Moon Sign Libra

This can be a relaxed time of imaginative meditation, healing and spiritual renewal. Strong ideas are working their way to the surface all the time and issues that seemed complicated only a day or two ago can now be quite easy to deal with. This is also a time when you may be doing all you can to help those who are less fortunate than yourself.

31 MONDAY
Moon Age Day 24   Moon Sign Libra

Look out for a high-spirited period when you are certainly going to be very popular. What better trends could anyone want for this particular day of the year? You might not feel very much like working today but when it comes to enjoying yourself the sky is the limit. You will be as bright as the fireworks tonight and just as wonderful.

How to Calculate Your Rising Sign

Most astrologers agree that, next to the Sun Sign, the most important influence on any person is the Rising Sign at the time of their birth. The Rising Sign represents the astrological sign that was rising over the eastern horizon when each and every one of us came into the world. It is sometimes also called the Ascendant.

Let us suppose, for example, that you were born with the Sun in the zodiac sign of Libra. This would bestow certain characteristics on you that are likely to be shared by all other Librans. However, a Libran with Aries Rising would show a very different attitude towards life, and of course relationships, than a Libran with Pisces Rising.

For these reasons, this book shows how your zodiac Rising Sign has a bearing on all the possible positions of the Sun at birth. Simply look through the Aries table opposite.

As long as you know your approximate time of birth the graph will show you how to discover your Rising Sign.

Look across the top of the graph of your zodiac sign to find your date of birth, and down the side for your birth time (I have used Greenwich Mean Time). Where they cross is your Rising Sign. Don't forget to subtract an hour (or two) if appropriate for Summer Time.

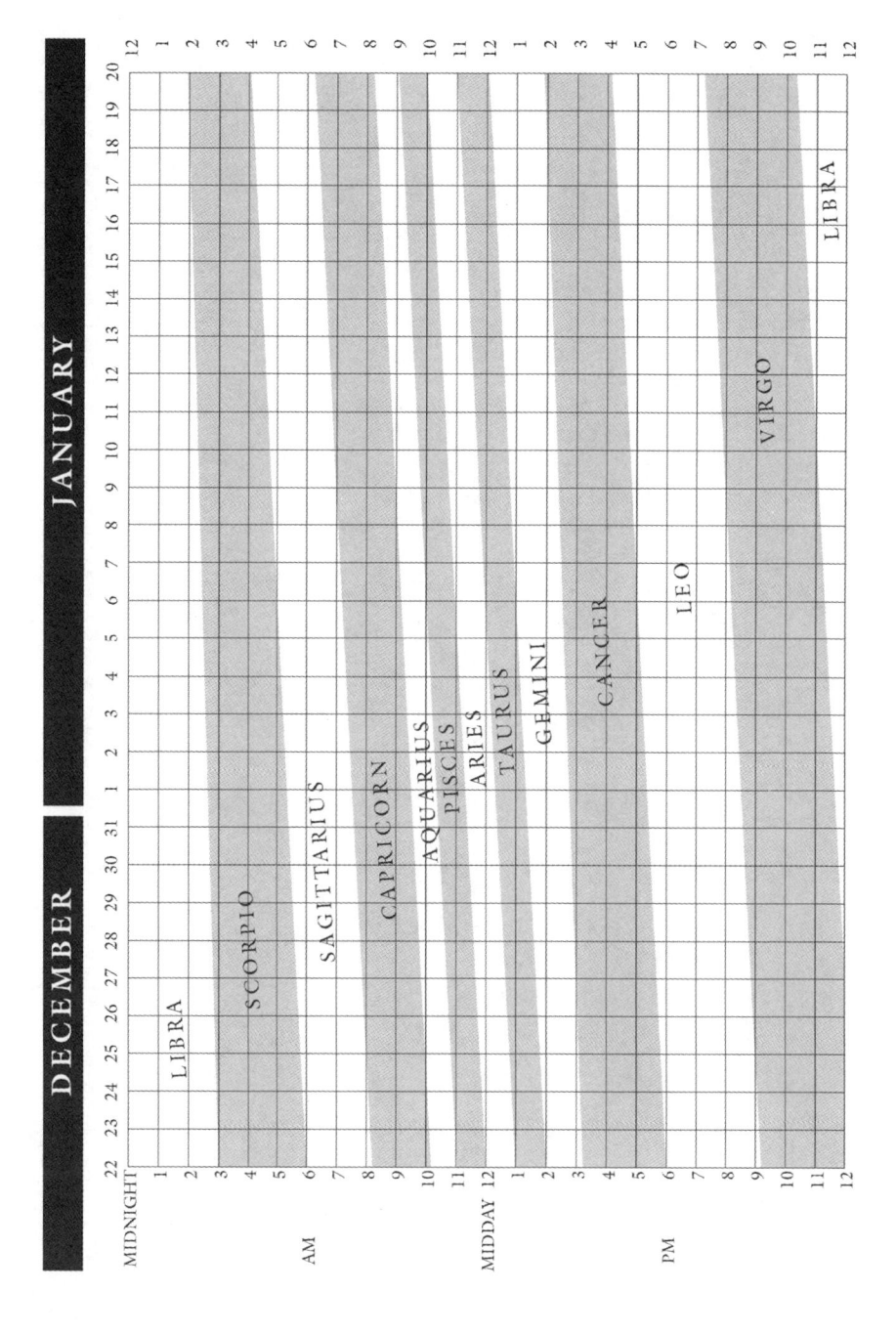

Rising Signs for Capricorn

THE ZODIAC, PLANETS AND CORRESPONDENCES

The Earth revolves around the Sun once every calendar year, so when viewed from Earth the Sun appears in a different part of the sky as the year progresses. In astrology, these parts of the sky are divided into the signs of the zodiac and this means that the signs are organised in a circle. The circle begins with Aries and ends with Pisces.

Taking the zodiac sign as a starting point, astrologers then work with all the positions of planets, stars and many other factors to calculate horoscopes and birth charts and tell us what the stars have in store for us.

The table below shows the planets and Elements for each of the signs of the zodiac. Each sign belongs to one of the four Elements: Fire, Air, Earth or Water. Fire signs are creative and enthusiastic; Air signs are mentally active and thoughtful; Earth signs are constructive and practical; Water signs are emotional and have strong feelings.

It also shows the metals and gemstones associated with, or corresponding with, each sign. The correspondence is made when a metal or stone possesses properties that are held in common with a particular sign of the zodiac.

Finally, the table shows the opposite of each star sign – this is the opposite sign in the astrological circle.

Placed	Sign	Symbol	Element	Planet	Metal	Stone	Opposite
1	Aries	Ram	Fire	Mars	Iron	Bloodstone	Libra
2	Taurus	Bull	Earth	Venus	Copper	Sapphire	Scorpio
3	Gemini	Twins	Air	Mercury	Mercury	Tiger's Eye	Sagittarius
4	Cancer	Crab	Water	Moon	Silver	Pearl	Capricorn
5	Leo	Lion	Fire	Sun	Gold	Ruby	Aquarius
6	Virgo	Maiden	Earth	Mercury	Mercury	Sardonyx	Pisces
7	Libra	Scales	Air	Venus	Copper	Sapphire	Aries
8	Scorpio	Scorpion	Water	Pluto	Plutonium	Jasper	Taurus
9	Sagittarius	Archer	Fire	Jupiter	Tin	Topaz	Gemini
10	Capricorn	Goat	Earth	Saturn	Lead	Black Onyx	Cancer
11	Aquarius	Waterbearer	Air	Uranus	Uranium	Amethyst	Leo
12	Pisces	Fishes	Water	Neptune	Tin	Moonstone	Virgo